Miracle Mornings

31 Days of Declarations and Devotions

By Rev. Dr. S. R. Watkins, Ph.D

Author of the five-part series, *"Life is a Test: Hope in a Confusing World"* and *"Biblical Economics 101: Living Under God's Financial Blessing."*

www.newstartministries.ca

Copyright © 2024 by New Start Ministries Ltd. All rights reserved. No part of this publication may be reproduced, stored in a retrieval system, or transmitted in any form or by any means - for example, electronic, photocopy, or recording without the publisher's prior written permission. The only exception is brief quotations in printed or digital reviews.
Scripture quotations are taken from the Amplified® Bible (AMPC),
Copyright © 1954, 1958, 1962, 1964, 1965, 1988 by The Lockman Foundation. Used by permission.
www.Lockman.org. Copyright © 2015 by The Lockman Foundation.
Scripture quotations identified NIV are from the Holy Bible, New International Version®. NIV®.
Copyright© 1973, 1978, 1984, 2011 by Biblical, Inc.TM. Used by permission of Zondervan. All rights reserved worldwide.
www.zondervan.com.
Scripture quotations marked MSG are taken from THE MESSAGE, Copyright © 1993, 2002, 2018 by Eugene H. Peterson. They are used with the permission of NavPress, represented by Tyndale House Publishers. All rights reserved and THE NEW KING JAMES VERSION, public domain.
All scripture quoted comes from the New International Version (NIV) unless otherwise stated.

Cover design by Cristina Valeria G. from Freelancer.com
Graphic design by Kris Nielson Design - www.krisdesign.ca

The comments and opinions expressed in this book are precisely that - "opinions" and opinions are never right or wrong - they are simply "opinions." It is not the intention of the author to coerce, force, or influence anyone other than to move them closer towards God. Further, it is not the intention of the author to solicit funds or donations (however, donations to this Ministry are appreciated, although tax receipts are unavailable). Suggested book reading/posters etc., are just that, "a suggestion." With a few exceptions, the author of this publication does not know the authors of the books that he is recommending.

Disclaimer: The author has taken great care to give due credit and acknowledge each quoted person. However, if you are an author whose work was mentioned in this book who has not been credited, and you would like us to either change, add your name or remove the copy in question, please email the author through the New Start Ministries website: www.newstartministries.ca

If this book is a blessing to you, and if you have comments or suggestions, please get in touch with the author at: info@newstartministries.ca

Dedication

I dedicate this book to the two people who helped me more than anyone else, and without them, this series of books that I have written in the last few years would never have been published. I am speaking, of course, of my editor, Graeme Henderson, whom I have nicknamed "Ed" (as in editor) for short. Ed has been instrumental. He has taken the rough-edged stone of my writing and polished it into a fine diamond. Of course, I shouldn't be so obstinate as to suggest it is "my writing" because as I have said throughout all of these books, it's about Holy Spirit and not me. I'm just His prophetic scribe, but His Words need to be put down on paper, and I need an editor to help me with that. Thank you, Graeme, you are the best, and I wish you every success in your Christian journey.

My friend, Anita Day, is probably the best proofreader I've ever met. She is downright picky, which is precisely what a person needs to be when they're proofreading. I am so glad that my books have blest you since you won't allow me to pay you; so, thanks and keep proofreading so that you can continue to be blest by these books! See you at the Ponoka Rodeo and "the Chucks"!

Reviews

"This book is great, rooted in the word of God, get your mind, focused on declaring what God says about what you were facing instead of declaring your problems."

Lorna Faith
Red Deer, Alberta

"I have used a lot of different types of devotional books over the course of my Christian life, but this one "takes the cake." It's exciting to open the book each morning and find out what the author is written about on a given day. It's quite invigorating! Definitely five stars!"

George Thomson
Santa Clara, California

5.0 out of 5 stars!
Order and Authority

"I'm one of those people who wakes up with everything that needs to happen that day on my mind. Kind of overload. **Miracle Mornings** *has been a fantastic way to get my mind in the right mode to see things from God's perspective and give order to my thoughts. It also helps me to stand in the authority Christ has given us to effectively live this life and not just be alive."*

Carol Crosson
Calgary, Alberta

Table of Contents

Notes 6

Acknowledgments 7

Introduction 8

How To Use This Book 19

Clarification 21

25 Bible Verses That You Just Need To Know! 23

Say This And Receive This Every Morning 27

Day One 28

Epilogue 90

Author's Note 96

My Decree Prayers 97

Decree The Word For Your Healing 101

Word Confessions 105

Releasing Prophetic Decrees 107

Who Is Doc? 110

Doc's Book Club 111

Favourite Authors 115

Additional Books By S. R. Watkins 116

Shopping And Seminars 123

Posters 125

Notes 128

Notes

I am a Canadian citizen living in sunny southern Alberta. We Canadians spell a few words differently from those in many other countries, as we often use British spelling practices. Examples include "colour," "favourite," "blest," "cheque," "saviour" and "centre." Out of respect for my Canadian heritage, I am retaining elements of Canadian culture in my writing style and the spelling of certain words.

I refuse to capitalize the name satan. I know that is grammatically incorrect, but satan doesn't deserve the honour, and besides, it's my book. He has done everything he can to stop its publication, so this is my revenge on him.

If you have not already noticed, you will see that I always refer to Holy Spirit as "Holy Spirit." I never refer to Him as "the Holy Spirit." That is because Holy Spirit is not a "thing" or an "it." Holy Spirit is a person - part of the Trinity of God (Father, Son, Holy Spirit). I do not believe that referring to Holy Spirit as "the" fits the person of God that Holy Spirit exemplifies.

One thing I've learned about book publishing is that selling books is all about marketing, and the best form of marketing is word of mouth, which comes from reviews and endorsements. If you enjoy this book of wisdom, I would greatly appreciate it if you could visit Amazon, Barnes & Noble, or Chapters/Indigo and leave a review. If you desire, an endorsement emailed to me would be greatly appreciated.

Please look at my website. You will find many "free things" like blogs, Bible studies, sermons, videos, book suggestions, etc.

Finally, please enjoy these Declarations! Personally, I use them every morning and read my "Life is a Test" books daily. May God shield you from all works of the enemy as you read, study, and grow towards Him (Eph. 6:10-18).

"Doc"
info@newstartministries.ca

"The purpose of life is to overcome the darkness that is in the Earth and help others to do that as well." Dr. S. R. Watkins

Acknowledgments

Thank you, Graeme Henderson, for your terrific editing. You are amazing, and I could not have completed ***"Miracle Mornings"*** without your wise input. We are a good team! Let's do more books!

Graeme dedicates much of his weekly time to empowering believers and reaching the lost around his home city of Nanaimo, British Columbia. He runs a website there as well to connect believers in the city: nanaimochristianconnect.com
If you would like to learn more or support his ministry, please email him directly at graemephenderson@gmail.com.

Thank you, Kris Nielson, for your usual great design and all the "extras" you do for me. You're the best! (design@krisdesign.ca)

Thank you, Anita Day, for proofreading the manuscript. Your diligence and "good eye" are appreciated.

Thank you, Cristina Valeria G., from www.freelancer.com, for your terrific cover designs! I highly recommend you!

I am so very grateful to my many friends and supporters who have bought and read my previous books, given me feedback, and written reviews. Thanks!

Introduction
The Great Confession: Unveiling the Spiritual Foundation of Christianity.

Christianity is often called the "Great Confession." Why? It is not merely a label but a profound acknowledgment of the transformative power of using God's spoken Words. In a nutshell, it is what Christianity and being a Christian is all about. Indeed, we cannot even become Christians unless we speak the Word of God out loud (Rom. 10:9) and confess what we believe and who we believe! The essence of this faith goes beyond rituals and doctrines, finding its roots in a heartfelt confession: sincerely believing in your heart what you speak with your mouth. This shapes the believer's identity and transcends any other natural experience, differentiating Christianity from all the world's religions. *

The Power of Words

God has repeatedly said in His Word (the Bible) that words - His Words possess an inherent power to shape reality. This foundational story comes from the Book of Genesis at the beginning of the Bible, where God Himself speaks creation into existence. According to the Canadian Oxford dictionary, "be" means "exist, live." In the Book of Genesis, God used the power of His Words to say the word "be," and "it" happened. The first of nine examples appears in *"Let there be light"* (verse 3) and "there was light." He spoke it, and it happened! Repeatedly, as we see from reading through the Holy Bible, in both the Old and New Testaments, we discover that the creative power of His Word extends beyond the act of creation to the transformative nature of confession in Christianity.

Today, in Christianity, we can be powerful voices and people of light or walk in the same rebellion that entered the heart of humanity in Genesis 3 and use our voices for evil. This, of course, begs a question. If God can do all He has done, why do we think we can match or rival Him in the pride of our hearts and actions? Who are we to say that we can hear from Him, speak His words, and know what's in His heart? Are we trying to become "God" or "like a god" by speaking out Words to change things? This is the breaking point for many denominations that would deem these actions heretical. This is where the so-called "word of faith movement" gets a "bad wrap."

Note: There is a long footnote to coincide with this page and I had placed it here. However, "Ed" suggested I move it to the end of this introduction. So, I did. Ed always knows what's best!

However, all one has to do is examine the scriptures for themselves and see how repeatedly they tell us the importance of using/speaking God's Words. Further, Jesus said that we, by using His Name, would do greater works than He did (John 14:12), and that's coming from a guy who raised people from the dead and walked on water! He did it and said that we could, too.

The concept of confession in Christianity is not limited to the mere acknowledgment of "confessing our sins" but extends to the affirmation of faith. The Apostle Paul says in Romans 10:9, *"If you declare with your mouth, 'Jesus is Lord,' and believe in your heart that God raised him from the dead, you will be saved."* This proclamation is not merely a vocalization but a profound confession that redefines one's spiritual identity and establishes a permanent connection with the Trinity (God the Father, Son, and Holy Spirit). In short, we cannot be saved without doing this very thing!

Confession as a Path to Redemption

Christianity acknowledges the sin and imperfections of humanity - the fact that every human being was born into sin (*"for all have sinned and fall short of the glory of God"* - Rom. 3:23), which, of course, requires and emphasizes the need for repentance and redemption. Confessing our sins is a pivotal step on the journey to spiritual renewal. Recognizing sin and confessing it is foundational to our relationship with God and the first step in our walk with Him. How was that connection made? Holy Spirit convicts us of sin and leads us toward Jesus. From there, Jesus said we cannot reach God the Father without going through Him first. *"Jesus answered, 'I am the way, truth, and life. No one comes to the Father except through me'"* (John 14:6). Muhammad didn't say that, nor did Buddha, the 10,000 Hindu gods, the New Age gods or any other demonic thing. Why? Because they can't. Both Mohammed and Buddha were men, not deities and not God. The 10,000 Hindu gods don't even exist other than being demons, and the same goes for the New Age gods or whatever they are. My point is that wisdom comes from truth and the only truth is Jesus. So, no, there are not dozens or hundreds of ways to find God. There is only one way, and that is through Jesus. This "Great Confession" (Rom. 10:9), as it is known, is not a burden but a liberating act that allows believers to unburden their souls and seek divine forgiveness, and from there have their lives completely transformed, leading to eternal life when their human bodies die.

This is further reiterated by Jesus, who was visited by an educated scholar named Nicodemus in the Book of John. Nicodemus could see that Jesus was a unique rabbi and an incredible teacher. He met with Jesus one night away from the rest of the religious people, so he would not be caught with Him. *"Now there was a Pharisee, a man named Nicodemus who was a member of the Jewish ruling council. He came to Jesus at night and said, 'Rabbi, we know that you are a teacher who has come from God. No one could perform the signs you are doing if God were not with him.' Jesus replied, 'Very truly, I tell you, no one can see the kingdom of God unless they are born again.' 'How can someone be born when they are old?' Nicodemus asked. 'Surely they cannot enter a second time into their mother's womb to be born!' Jesus answered, 'Very truly I tell you, no one can enter the kingdom of God unless they are born of water and the Spirit. Flesh gives birth to flesh, but the Spirit gives birth to spirit. You should not be surprised at my saying, 'You must be born again.' The wind blows wherever it pleases. You hear its sound, but you cannot tell where it comes from or where it is going. So it is with everyone born of the Spirit'"* (John 3:1-8).

How do we do what Jesus tells us to? Become born again!

1. Recognizing that all have sinned and fallen short of the glory of God, including you and me! (Rom. 3:23)
2. Coming to Jesus and wanting to confess that sin (James 5:16; 1 John 1:9).
3. Willing to open our hearts to receive Him and to have His clean Blood washed through our sinful blood (Eph. 1:7).
4. Believing that Jesus is Lord and confessing that! (Rom. 10:9)
5. Making a firm decision to turn from our way of the past, and from this day forward, walk in full communion and fellowship with Jesus, and the comforter known as Holy Spirit, who Jesus sent to us (2 Cor. 5:17; Gal. 2:20).
6. Knowing that the wages of sins are eternal death, we have eternal life by doing all the above (Rom. 8:23).

You will notice how many of these steps involve believing in your heart and speaking out words. Just as God created the world in Genesis 1, we make a new world (life) for ourselves by believing, speaking, and repenting (repentance of sin means to stop doing it!) In the Gospel of Matthew, Jesus invites His followers to confess their sins, assuring them of God's mercy. Matt. 11:28-30 echoes this sentiment, *"Come to me, all you who are weary and burdened, and I will give you rest."* Confessing sins is not meant to induce guilt but to usher in a transformative experience in which the individual is cleansed by the Blood of Jesus, who died on the cross to save all of mankind so that we might be born again into the great Kingdom of God.

Identity and Purpose in Confession

Christianity views confession as a means of affirming a person's identity and purpose, indeed, why they were even born. The Apostle Peter's confession in Matthew 16:16, in which he declares Jesus the Messiah, *"the Son of the living God,"* exemplifies this profound act of acknowledgment. In this instance, the confession becomes pivotal (his own "epiphany moment"), setting Peter on a path of discipleship and purpose for his life.

The Great Confession, therefore, is not merely a repetition of words but a heartfelt acknowledgment that establishes a personal connection with God Almighty, maker of heaven and earth. Through this act, we affirm our identity as children of God and find purpose, salvation, power and authority in the teachings of Jesus Christ. The confession becomes a transformative force that shapes individual character, guides believers on their spiritual journey, and grants them entrance into the Kingdom of God. If I were to summarize all the scriptures, Old and New Testaments, into one word, I would use "alignment" (aka alignment with God).

Unity in Confession

Despite its diverse denominations and theological opinions, Christianity is unified by a common foundation: the Great Confession. The Nicene Creed, a widely accepted statement of Christian faith, is a testament to this unity. The creed begins with *"We believe,"* underscoring a collective confession that transcends individual differences and denominational boundaries.

The Great Confession is not a one-time event but a continuous spiritual discipline that becomes part of the soul and foundation of the Christian life. The Apostle Paul, in his letters, encourages believers to confess their faith not only through words but also through their actions. In Philippians 2:11, he states, *"and every tongue acknowledge that Jesus Christ is Lord, to the glory of God the Father."* This goes far beyond the church walls and into the everyday lives of believers. It manifests in acts of love, compassion, and service to others. That is why

Jesus said we were to serve others and not be His servants: *"You are my friends if you do what I command. I no longer call you servants because a servant does not know his master's business. Instead, I have called you friends, for everything I learned from my Father I have made known to you. You did not choose me, but I chose you and appointed you so that you might go and bear fruit (fruit that will last) and so that whatever you ask in my name, the Father will give you"* (John 15:14-16).

As a spiritual discipline, the Great Confession challenges believers to live out their faith in a tangible way, bearing witness to the entire world of the transformative power of living our lives for Jesus. Once we know this and live like this, we are to take this incredible experience of a new life, the Word of God itself, and go out into the world to *"make disciples of all men"* (Matt. 28:19).

From a spiritual perspective, the words "confession" and "profession" share certain similarities, particularly in personal growth, self-awareness, and aligning one's actions with God's higher principles. Here are some points of similarity from a biblical perspective:

Confession:

- Involves acknowledging and admitting our mistakes or wrongdoings.
- Is a process of self-reflection and awareness of our shortcomings.
- Emphasizes transparency and authenticity by openly admitting our faults or sins.
- Involves a sincere acknowledgment of our imperfections.
- Is seen as a transformative process where we seek forgiveness and strive for personal growth and spiritual improvement.
- Acknowledges a divine presence and recognizes the need for God's mercy.

Profession:

- Is like the confession concept as it involves self-awareness, but it focuses on openly declaring and affirming our beliefs, values, and commitment to God's principles.
- Involves transparency and authenticity but in the context of expressing our spiritual allegiance.
- Involves acknowledging God as God, Jesus as the King of Kings and Lord of Lords, and Holy Spirit as our divine comforter.
- Implies taking responsibility for our spiritual journey, adhering to the Word of God in His Holy Scriptures, and living by those principles.

Creation and Declaration

From the beginning (literally, in Genesis, chapter 1, and continuing) two words stand as pillars, each carrying profound spiritual significance - "create" and "declaration." God spoke (declared) and He created. These terms are intricately woven into the whole foundation of Christianity, revealing the divine essence of God's interaction with the world.

At the heart of Christian doctrine lies the concept of creation, a God-ordained act, because, without God, there is nothing. He created *"the heavens and the earth"* (Gen. 1:1). The term "create" in this context signifies the majestic unfolding of God's plan, where He brought the universe into existence from nothingness. Creation is an act of divine love, a manifestation of God's boundless creativity, wisdom, and sovereignty.

As Christians, we find ourselves immersed in awe and wonder at the intricacies of the natural world. Each creature, from the smallest ant to the mightiest mountain, bears the fingerprints of God. The act of creation reveals not only the grandeur of God but also His intimate involvement in every facet of existence, including every detail of our lives and the depth of His love for us. Why wouldn't He? We are His children; He created every one of us, which is why it breaks His heart when we walk away from Him and fall into sin. John 1:11 says, *"He came to His own, and His own did not receive Him."* And so, He wept. This broke His heart, and it still does today. View the created world as a sacred gift, a testament to God's generosity and love. Romans 1:19 says that there is no excuse for not knowing God.

The term "declaration" takes on a different context. The Bible is consistent with declarations - divine proclamations of truth, purpose, and revelation. God's declarations are not arbitrary. They carry the weight of His authority and speak to the very core of human existence. From the Ten Commandments to the Sermon on the Mount, these declarations guide believers on the path of righteousness and illuminate a deeper relationship with God. The Psalms, for instance, are poetic declarations that resonate with the human soul, offering solace, encouragement, and hope. The Book of Proverbs demonstrates wisdom and how to live this God-ordained life that He has blest us with.

As Christians, we believe that the ultimate declaration of God's love and redemption came through the person of Jesus Christ, His Son, who was born and died for us. The Word became flesh (John 1:14), and God declared His plan for salvation in Christ. The cross is the ultimate declaration of God's sacrificial love, inviting humanity into a restored relationship. Why? God does not tolerate sin of any nature and, therefore, it must be disposed of, or as the Bible says, "atoned." Something or someone must take the place of the sin that we humans create. *"For God so loved the world, that he gave his only begotten Son, that whosoever believeth in him should not perish, but have everlasting life"* (John 3:16).

How and why did that happen? In the Old Testament, people would have to kill animals and use the blood to wash away their sins. Jesus became the sacrificial "lamb of God that takes away the sin of the world" (John 1:29), and through His death on the cross, we are made clean. Of course, only if we believe in our heart and speak with our mouth (confess) that Jesus is Lord! (Rom. 10:9) So, no matter how we "slice it and dice it," confessing words with the subsequent accompanying actions is the foundation of our relationship with God.

The Power of Decree and Declaration

As the foundational text of Christianity, the Bible offers numerous verses highlighting word potency. Prov. 18:21 asserts, *"Death and life are in the power of the tongue, and those who love it will eat its fruits."* This wisdom underscores the importance that words play in shaping our lives. Additionally, in Mark 11:23, Jesus Himself emphasizes the power of faith-filled words, saying, *"Truly, I say to you, whoever says to this mountain, 'Be taken up and thrown into the sea,' and does not doubt in his heart, but believes that what he says will come to pass, it will be done for him."*

These verses provide a biblical foundation for decreeing and declaring. Christians are encouraged to speak Words of faith, aligning their declarations with God's promises and will. By doing so, believers actively co-create their reality with God, leveraging His power by agreeing with His Words.

Decreeing and declaring the Word of God is not merely a vocal exercise but a spiritual discipline that engages the heart and mind. Romans 10:17 affirms, *"So faith comes from hearing, and hearing through the word of Christ."* By consistently hearing God's Word (hear it by speaking it out loud!) we strengthen our faith and cultivate a deeper intimacy with God. This practice is a powerful tool for spiritual empowerment, aligning individuals with the truth of their identity in Christ. Ephesians 1:3

reminds believers of their spiritual inheritance, *"Blessed be the God and Father of our Lord Jesus Christ, who has blest us in Christ with every spiritual blessing in the heavenly places."* By decreeing and declaring God's promises, we actively access and claim these blessings. This spiritual empowerment is a source of strength, resilience, and victory over life's challenges.

Further, we must take into consideration several essential foundational scriptures:

- God said to Moses, *"I AM WHO I AM. This is what you are to say to the Israelites: 'I AM has sent me to you'"* (Ex. 3:14).

- *"I am the Lord, and there is no other; apart from me there is no God"* (Is. 45:5).

- *"So is my word that goes out from my mouth: It will not return to me empty, but will accomplish what I desire and achieve the purpose for which I sent it"* (Is. 55:11).

- *"You are to speak to him and put the words in his mouth; and I, even I, will be with your mouth and his mouth, and I will teach you what you are to do"* (Ex. 4:15).

- *"If anyone speaks, they should do so as one who speaks the very words of God. If anyone serves, they should do so with the strength God provides so that in all things, God may be praised through Jesus Christ. To him be the glory and the power forever and ever. Amen"* (1 Peter 4:11).

- *"I can do all things through him who strengthens me"* (Phil. 4:13).

Decreeing and declaring the Word of God facilitates a harmonious alignment with God's divine purpose for individuals. Jer. 29:11 declares, *"'For I know the plans I have for you,' declares the Lord, 'plans to prosper you and not to harm you, plans to give you hope and a future.'"*

By consistently affirming God's promises over our lives, we reinforce our commitment to God's purpose, maintaining a mindset attuned to Holy Spirit. Furthermore, this practice helps believers resist negative influences and confess their faith in the face of adversity. Proclaiming God's Word reinforces the truth that, despite external circumstances, God's promises remain unshakable and reliable. *"Stand, therefore stand..."* (Eph. 6:14).

How do we do this?

It is good to take scriptures, paraphrase them in the first person, and declare them over us. Try these:

- "For I know the plans that you have for me, Lord, plans to prosper me and not to harm me, plans to give me hope and a future" (Jer. 29:11).

- "By His stripes, I am healed" (1 Peter 2:24).

- "No weapon formed against me shall prosper, And every tongue which rises against me in judgement I shall condemn. This is the heritage of the servants of the Lord, And their righteousness is from Him, says the Lord" (Is. 54:17).

By proclaiming these verses and others, we acknowledge God's sovereignty, faithfulness, and the transformative power of His Word.

Spiritual Warfare

Declaring the Word of God is also seen as a form of spiritual warfare. Ephesians 6:12 tells us that our struggle is *"not against flesh and blood but against spiritual forces of evil."* By speaking God's Word, we engage in a spiritual battle, affirming our identity as children of God and standing against the enemy's lies and deceptions. In the Gospel of Matthew, Jesus provides a powerful example of using Scripture to resist temptation during His forty days in the wilderness (Matthew 4:1-11). This underscores the importance of relying on the Word of God as a weapon against spiritual attacks. By declaring God's Word, we actively participate in the ongoing spiritual warfare, trusting in the authority and power of God's spoken Word.

Faith and Confession

Hebrews 11:1 defines faith as *"the substance of things hoped for, the evidence of things not seen."* When Christians declare the Word of God, they exercise faith by trusting in the unseen promises of God. Romans 10:17 affirms that faith comes by us hearing the Word of God. Therefore, declaring God's Word becomes a catalyst for building and strengthening faith.

Declaring the Word of God over oneself is a central aspect of the Christian faith, grounded in biblical principles and spiritual insights. By grounding this practice in the Scriptures, engaging in spiritual warfare, and expressing faith through confession, we align our lives with God's truth, experience transformation in our spiritual journey, and become a new man, for the old man has passed away, (2 Cor. 5:17) and now we have power and authority as we walk in the Kingdom of God, which is here on the Earth. The Kingdom of God is a government, God's government, here on earth, and we have entrance to it once we believe in our hearts and speak with our mouths that Jesus is Lord! The declaration of God's Word is a powerful tool for us to experience the abundant life Jesus promised and to navigate the world's challenges with unwavering faith.

Summary

Remember, *"faith comes by hearing, and hearing by the Word of God"* (Rom. 10:17, NKJV). To build strong and unwavering faith, speak the Word of God aloud to your challenges, and watch in faith as His power manifests in your life.

The Word of God is rich with meaning, encompassing both *logos* and *rhema*. Logos refers to the written Word, while rhema signifies the spoken Word. Immerse yourself in the logos, the written scriptures, and allow Holy Spirit to quicken specific verses to your heart for your unique circumstances. As you speak these verses aloud, they transform into rhema, the spoken Word of God, which empowers you with the faith needed to fulfill your desires.

This is how you overcome challenges and discouragement - by declaring His all-powerful, life-giving Word as seeds you are planting. *"The seed is the Word of God"* (Luke 8:11). When you follow this divine plan, you give God something to work with on your behalf. As He promises in Isaiah 55:10-12:

"For as the rain comes down, and the snow from heaven, and do not return there, but water the earth, And make it bring forth and bud, that it may give seed to the sower and bread to the eater, So shall My word be that goes forth from My mouth; It shall not return to Me void, But it shall accomplish what I please, And it shall prosper in the thing for which I sent it."

As you learn to walk by faith and not by sight, embrace the wonderful promises God has given you in His Word - they are all for you. If doubts creep in, overcome them by obeying and declaring the Word of God. Read it, and speak it out loud, allowing His truth to fill your heart and mind.

Footnote: From page 1 of this introduction:

* "Religion" and Christianity are polar opposites. All religions (and Christianized cults) have one thing in common: a person must do something to appease some deity to be accepted. Christianity is different in every way. There is nothing you can do to get favour from God. We are saved by grace, not by works, which is the opposite of religion. In the broader sense of the term, religion can mean anything that you are obsessed with and keeps you from God. There's a joke that says that Canada's national religion is hockey! People in world religions are coming to their senses - whatever "god(s)" they believe in are not there. Buddha, Mohammed or any of the thousands of Hindu "gods" do not heal; they do not set people free or give eternal life in heaven; they don't do anything because, in the case of Hindu gods, they don't exist, and in the case of Buddha or Mohammed, any divine powers they claim to have, do not exist. Both Buddha and Mohammed were just men who are both dead and in hell. Buddha even prophesied the coming of Jesus. Satan is alive and well and, through his blinders, will convince people to believe in a variety of dead and non-existent gods.

How To Use This Book.

It's simple. Believe in your heart and speak with your mouth the Word of God. In short, the following pages contain 31 days of scriptures and devotions. Use this book as your morning devotional before your feet hit the floor. In addition, I would always encourage you to have your own daily Bible study, preferably at the start of the day; if that doesn't fit your schedule, get up earlier or do it before you go to bed. Here is what I do:

1. Upon waking up in the morning, I first praise God. I'm alive! My name is not in the obituary column in today's newspaper! (I often check just to make sure!) I continue giving Him praise and glory for several minutes, listing everything I am thankful for.

2. I read several daily devotionals, including my own five *"Life is a Test"* books.

3. Next, I spend some time speaking declarations and decrees using my book - this one! I also decree Psalms 91 and 103 every day.

4. Finally, I finish the time by reading two chapters of the Old Testament, one of the New Testament, and perhaps a Psalm or Proverb.

This will be the easy part of your day once it becomes routine. The tricky part is remembering everything you've prayed about, everything you've decreed and declared, etc., throughout the day. No sooner do we get downstairs with the family, start driving to work, speak on the phone, etc., than we become like Dr. Jekyll and Mr. Hyde - different people. How to combat that? Joshua handled it quite nicely in verse eight of the first chapter of his book. *"Meditate on this word day and night, and then you will be prosperous."*

Rather than "reinvent the wheel" the following 3 paragraphs are from my book *"Life is a Test: Hope in a Confusing World"* Volume 1, July 23.

"Meditate on His Word. (Jos. 1:8)

I emphasize the importance of the Word of God in the Bible because it is an operation manual. If all else fails, just read the book of instructions! I tell the students in my seminars not to "read" the Bible but to study or meditate on it.

In the original Greek, "meditate" means "think deeply or focus one's mind for some time." In other words, study! Memorize it. Ponder it. Let it sink in.

"Meditate" also means to "mutter." So, throughout the day, "mutter" to yourself. Speak in tongues or speak the Word out. Talk to God (and listen too) as if He were your best friend standing right next to you because, guess what? He is! Before you spend money on anything, ask Him. Ask Him to help you be a good steward of the blessings that He has sent you.

The norm for me, when I go shopping, is to get deals and discounts. It happens so frequently that I expect it to happen. Why? Because I'm in constant contact with Him, He guides and directs me all the time (assuming I keep the connection open)!" *

One last thought. I have used another type of decree book for years. **"Heaven Declares: Prophetic Decrees to Start Your Day"** by Dr. Hakeem Collins. This is an amazing book! Published by Destiny Image in the USA. Buy a copy!

---

* ***"Life is a Test: Hope in a Confusing World"*** is a five-part series available from Amazon, Chapters, Indigo, Barnes and Noble or order from your favourite bookstore. 5 Star Reviews!

Clarification!

In recent years, the Charismatic and Pentecostal movements have seen a rise in speaking decrees and declarations. While declaring God's promises holds power, there's a danger when such proclamations are made without Spirit-led discernment!

Declarations, when made presumptuously, lack the grounding needed in faith and discernment. True authority doesn't come from merely holding a title (apostle), for example, and/or "naming it and claiming it" without these words aligning with God's will. Romans 4:17 calls for *"those things that are not as though they were,"* as Abraham did, but remember that Abraham's faith was anchored in God's specific promise, not his own words. Similarly, when Jesus cursed the fig tree (Mark 11:12-14), He was moved by a divine sense cultivated through His deep relationship with the Father. His actions flowed from an intimate knowledge of God's purposes, not arbitrary power.

Intercession differs from declarations in its sacrificial nature and depth. Rather than speaking at a situation, intercession means "standing in the gap," aligning ourselves with God's intentions through prayer. In Romans 8:26-27, Holy Spirit intercedes for us, guiding our prayers and opening our understanding of God's will. Declarations can become empty without the backing of heaven's authority and without this discernment.

Declarations rooted in human desire can drift from God's will. Jesus teaches in Mark 11:23-24 to speak with faith, but this faith is not mere optimism; it's a conviction rooted in God's spoken Word. Romans 10:17 reminds us, *"Faith comes by hearing, and hearing by the word of God."* Actual authority to declare arises from time spent in God's presence, not shortcuts!

Spirit-led declarations spring from "Spirit-induced faith," a faith kindled by Holy Spirit's leading. When declarations align with God's heart, they carry divine power. When they don't, people speak out of their souls. Jesus modelled this, commanding miracles only after time spent in solitude and prayer, emphasizing that authority flows from relationships, not formulas.

The church today must discern between decrees and intercession, realizing that while declarations have power, they should arise from Spirit-filled intercession. As we recover the art of waiting on God, listening for His voice, and allowing His will to shape our prayers, our words will be endowed with the authority to bring heaven's will to earth. Only then will our declarations genuinely carry the weight of heaven and fulfill God's purpose. In short, faith-filled decrees and declarations must come after much prayer, fasting, intercession, Bible study, waiting on the Lord, hearing from the Lord, etc.

The purpose of this book is not for you to simply shout passages out every morning before you get out of bed. Speaking the Scriptures is not a quick fix for life's problems, and it is not a demand we place on God, using Him as our errand boy. All these decrees and declarations come forth after earnest prayer! Find the promises in the Word for things you need (like healing, for example), fast and pray into this; that's the intercession part. Only then can you speak out the Word of God over your situation with proper authority and alignment.

25 Bible Verses That You Just Need To Know! (NKJV)

"For God so loved the world that He gave His only begotten Son, that whoever believes in Him should not perish but have everlasting life. For God did not send His Son into the world to condemn the world, but that the world through Him might be saved. He who believes in Him is not condemned; but he who does not believe is condemned already, because he has not believed in the name of the only begotten Son of God. And this is the condemnation, that the light has come into the world, and men loved darkness rather than light, because their deeds were evil. For everyone practicing evil hates the light and does not come to the light, lest his deeds should be exposed. But he who does the truth comes to the light, that his deeds may be clearly seen, that they have been done in God" (John 3:16-21).

"All Scripture is given by inspiration of God, and is profitable for doctrine, for reproof, for correction, for instruction in righteousness" (2 Tim. 3:16).

"For the word of God is living and powerful, and sharper than any two-edged sword, piercing even to the division of soul and spirit, and of joints and marrow, and is a discerner of the thoughts and intents of the heart" (Heb. 4:12).

"Keep this Book of the Law always on your lips; meditate on it day and night, so that you may be careful to do everything written in it. Then you will be prosperous and successful" (Jos. 1:8).

"Sanctify them by Your truth. Your word is truth" (John 17:17).

"So is my word that goes out from my mouth: It will not return to me empty, but will accomplish what I desire and achieve the purpose for which I sent it" (Is. 55:11).

"Therefore lay aside all filthiness and overflow of wickedness, and receive with meekness the implanted word, which is able to save your souls. But be doers of the word, and not hearers only, deceiving yourselves" (James 1:21-22).

"So then faith comes by hearing, and hearing by the word of God" (Rom. 10:17).

"For as the rain comes down, and the snow from heaven, And do not return there, But water the earth, And make it bring forth and bud, That it may give seed to the sower And bread to the eater, So shall My word be that goes forth from My mouth; It shall not return to Me void, But it shall accomplish what I please, And it shall prosper in the thing for which I sent it" (Is. 55:10-11).

"For the message of the cross is foolishness to those who are perishing, but to us who are being saved it is the power of God" (1 Cor. 1:18).

"This Book of the Law shall not depart from your mouth, but you shall meditate in it day and night, that you may observe to do according to all that is written in it. For then you will make your way prosperous, and then you will have good success" (Jos. 1:8).

"And Joshua said to the people, "Sanctify yourselves, for tomorrow the Lord will do wonders among you" (Jos. 3:5).

"If My people who are called by My name will humble themselves, and pray and seek My face, and turn from their wicked ways, then I will hear from heaven, and will forgive their sin and heal their land" (2 Chron. 7:14).

"But you will receive power when the Holy Spirit comes on you; and you will be my witnesses in Jerusalem, and in all Judea and Samaria, and to the ends of the earth" (Acts 1:8).

"In the last days, God says, I will pour out my Spirit on all people. Your sons and daughters will prophesy, your young men will see visions, your old men will dream dreams" (Acts 2:17).

"He sent His word and healed them, And delivered them from their destructions" (Ps. 107:20).

"For I am not ashamed of the gospel of Christ, for it is the power of God to salvation for everyone who believes, for the Jew first and also for the Greek" (Rom. 1:16).

"In the beginning was the Word, and the Word was with God, and the Word was God. He was in the beginning with God. All things were made through Him, and without Him nothing was made that was made. In Him was life, and the life was the light of men. And the light shines in the darkness, and the darkness did not comprehend it" (John 1:1-5).

"The word is near you, in your mouth and in your heart" (that is, the word of faith which we preach): that if you confess with your mouth the Lord Jesus and believe in your heart that God has raised Him from the dead, you will be saved. For with the heart one believes unto righteousness, and with the mouth confession is made unto salvation" (Rom. 10:8-10).

"For the wrath of God is revealed from heaven against all ungodliness and unrighteousness of men, who suppress the truth in unrighteousness, because what may be known of God is manifest in them, for God has shown it to them. For since the creation of the world His invisible attributes are clearly seen, being understood by the things that are made, even His eternal power and Godhead, so that they are without excuse, because, although they knew God, they did not glorify Him as God, nor were thankful, but became futile in their thoughts, and their foolish hearts were darkened. Professing to be wise, they became fools, and changed the glory of the incorruptible God into an image made like corruptible man - and birds and four-footed animals and creeping things" (Rom. 1:18-23).

"Stand therefore, having girded your waist with truth, having put on the breastplate of righteousness, and having shod your feet with the preparation of the gospel of peace; above all, taking the shield of faith with which you will be able to quench all the fiery darts of the wicked one. And take the helmet of salvation, and the sword of the Spirit, which is the word of God; praying always with all prayer and supplication in the Spirit, being watchful to this end with all perseverance and supplication for all the saints and for me, that utterance may be given to me, that I may open my mouth boldly to make known the mystery of the gospel, for which I am an ambassador in chains; that in it I may speak boldly, as I ought to speak" (Eph. 6:10-13).

"And Jesus came and spoke to them, saying, "All authority has been given to Me in heaven and on earth. Go therefore and make disciples of all the nations, baptizing them in the name of the Father and of the Son and of the Holy Spirit, teaching them to observe all things that I have commanded you; and lo, I am with you always, even to the end of the age" (Matt: 28:18-20).

"Jesus replied, 'Very truly I tell you, no one can see the kingdom of God unless they are born again" (John 3:3).

"But even if our gospel is veiled, it is veiled to those who are perishing, whose minds the god of this age has blinded, who do not believe, lest the light of the gospel of the glory of Christ, who is the image of God, should shine on them. For we do not preach ourselves, but Christ Jesus the Lord, and ourselves your bondservants for Jesus' sake. For it is the God who commanded light to shine out of darkness, who has shone in our hearts to give the light of the knowledge of the glory of God in the face of Jesus Christ" (2 Cor. 4:3-6).

"Finally, my brethren, be strong in the Lord and in the power of His might. Put on the whole armour of God, that you may be able to stand against the wiles of the devil. For we do not wrestle against flesh and blood, but against principalities, against powers, against the rulers of the darkness of this age, against spiritual hosts of wickedness in the heavenly places. Therefore take up the whole armour of God, that you may be able to withstand in the evil day, and having done all, to stand"

(Eph. 6:10-13).

Say This Every Morning!

"Heavenly Father, it is my choice to be a forgiving person. Therefore, I release into your hands all of my hurt, bitterness, anger and pain. I further release into Your hands all my judgments and all those who abused me in any way. I leave them all with You, Father. For you are trustworthy and good. In the Name of Jesus. Amen."

Receive This Every Morning!

"Every demon that has sought to torment me, every devil that has whispered lies into my spirit, and every satanic assignment aimed at my destiny has been CANCELLED in the mighty Name of Jesus! The chains of darkness that have held me captive are being shattered now, as the light of God's truth penetrates every shadow of despair.

I know that every work of witchcraft, every curse spoken against me, and every plot devised in the secret places has been returned to the sender. The arrows meant for me shall fall to the ground, for the Lord is my shield and your fortress. No weapon formed against me shall prosper, and every tongue that rises against me in judgment is condemned.

This is my season of divine reversal! The enemies that have pursued me have met their end. I am being lifted from the ashes of oppression into the brilliance of God's grace and favour. I expect a turnaround in every area of my life, for the heavens are open, and blessings are being poured out like never before.

I am a child of the Most High God, and no darkness can overshadow the light within me. I walk boldly in the authority given to me, reclaiming my peace, my joy, and your purpose Lord, for me. The battle is not mine, but the Lord's, and He has fought for me, securing my victory."

    In the last 20 years of my association with Glory of Zion in Corinth, Texas, I've had the distinct pleasure of meeting Dr. Odilia Leal. Odilia is an incredible, unique and mighty woman of God. I have learned that there's nothing more powerful in the universe than that of an intercessory, praying woman who takes her job very seriously. That's what she does. I once had "an audience" with her, and she gave me some fascinating and powerful advice. She told me to decree and declare the words "Davar shalom" seven times after praying and/or decreeing. "Davar" is Hebrew for "to speak" and "shalom" means "peace," and the number seven is the number of completion and perfection. She said that miracles begin to happen when you decree this or pray it over someone seven times. Sounds like great advice to me!

Day 1

MIRACLE MORNINGS

I walk in extraordinary energy and strength. My body is strong and fights off sickness and disease. My vision is keen, my mind is sharp, and my spirit is awake, charged with Holy Spirit and ready to walk through every door of favour and influence that God unfolds before me. As I speak in my spirit language, I rekindle the spiritual fire within me through the divine prayers of Holy Spirit. I am full of life and vitality, and my immune system is alive and thriving. I am a Godly spiritual force to reckon with! I live and walk in divine miracles. I run without weariness. I walk without fainting and fulfill my calling with unwavering energy. I am not merely surviving, I am thriving, propelled by the divine dynamo within me, generating extraordinary strength. When I walk into a room, the presence of God is there because I am there!

"You shall receive power when the Holy Ghost comes upon you, and you shall be my witnesses in Jerusalem, Judea, Samaria, and the uttermost parts of the earth" (Acts 1:8).

I am a powerhouse for God's glory, radiating the light of Jesus that illuminates the world. Bold and courageous, I operate in the Gifts of the Spirit, and through them my very presence preaches the gospel and makes disciples of all me (Matt. 28:19). I am a nation-changer, standing firm under pressure and my testimony ignites revival. My words transform the atmosphere, and I continually speak with newfound authority, causing demons to flee, Angels to be released, and the Kingdom of God to advance.

"If you can believe, all things are possible for him who believes" (Mark 9:23 MSG). And yes, I do believe!

Boundless blessings and increase are the norm for me. Why? Because I am a child of the living God who wants me blest going in and blest going out (Deut. 28:6). So, I am! Abundant provision flows into my life, enabling me to fulfill my needs and missions. I get deals and discounts all the time. God's blessings overflow, restoring sevenfold what the enemy has stolen. This is my season. I am a 100-fold believer.

Day 1

MIRACLE MORNINGS

"And it shall come to pass in the last day, says God, that I will pour out my Spirit on all flesh; your sons and your daughters shall prophesy, your young men shall see visions, and your old men shall dream dreams" (Acts 2:17).

"The voice of the Lord will shatter the enemy" (Is. 30:31).

"Believe the prophets, and you will prosper" (2 Chron. 20:20). Yes, I do prosper, because that is the will of God.

I prophesy the Word of the Lord over my life, home, family, city, and nation. I engage in spiritual warfare, wielding the prophecies that precede me. I release my faith and declare that the prophecies given to me have come to pass. My voice will function as the sword of the Lord, declaring His justice on earth. The voice of the Lord in my mouth shatters the enemy. I embrace God's prophetic voice, prospering, advancing, breaking out, breaking through, and achieving success. I am God's voice to my generation.

"God kept releasing a flow of extraordinary miracles through the hands of Paul" (Acts 19:11).

I decree miracles and release miracles to others. I am chosen by God to be a miracle worker. My hands are instruments of healing, bringing recovery to the sick. My words generate supernatural power, setting captives free and even raising the dead. This is my day of divine reversal, carrying the anointing to turn circumstances to God's glory.

"My grace is sufficient for you, for my strength will be made perfect in your weakness" (2 Cor. 12:9).

"If you diligently heed the voice of the Lord your God and do what is right in His sight, give ear to His commandments and keep all His statutes, I will put none of the diseases on you which I have brought on the Egyptians. For I am the Lord who heals you" (Ex. 15:26).

This is my year of destiny!

Day 2 — Miracle Mornings

In the Name of Jesus, by the authority of God's Word, I no longer look at myself through natural eyes but through the lens of God's Word. I am highly favoured by the Lord, crowned with glory and honour. I assert authority over condemnation, guilt, shame, and inferiority. These are not of God, and I break their power over me because they have no right or authority to be in my life.

In the Name of Jesus, I declare that I walk in favour and blessing in every way as I continually experience preferential treatment. Not only from God the Father but from others as well. I am blest going in and blest going out (Deut. 28:6). Condemnation has no place in my life (Rom. 8:1). From this moment onward, my self-esteem and self-image shall rise in alignment with God's Word. While I walk in humility, (Matt. 23:11-12) I acknowledge who I am in Christ and anticipate the treatment afforded to those who are highly favoured (Prov. 8:35). I also acknowledge and accept the reality that as a child of God, I am walking in abundant authority, (Col. 2:10) and as a result, I am healed, sanctified, blest, anointed, praised and prosperous by the Blood of the Lamb.

In the Name of Jesus, I declare that today is the day that the Lord has made (Ps. 118:24). I rejoice and I am glad in it and walk in continuing favour and blessing! Doors deemed impossible to open yield before me because divine favour paves the way. Fear, judgmentalism, and lovelessness have no place in my walk in life. I will continue to guard, keep, and occupy until Jesus comes.

"So Jesus answered and said to them, "Have faith in God. For assuredly, I say to you, whoever says to this mountain, 'Be removed and be cast into the sea,' and does not doubt in his heart, but believes that those things he says will be done, he will have whatever he says. Therefore I say to you, whatever things you ask when you pray, believe that you receive them, and you will have them" (Mark 11:23-24). Therefore, I address the mountains of _____, casting them into the sea!

"You will seek Me, and you will find Me when you seek Me with all your heart" (Jer. 29:12).

Day 2

MIRACLE MORNINGS

- I bind and remove poverty and debt, releasing prosperity and financial freedom.
- I bind the spirit of fear, sickness, and harm, releasing total health and divine protection.
- I bind hopelessness and depression, releasing hope and a sound mind.
- I bind the spirits stealing my clarity and future and release a clear vision from the Lord.
- I decree and declare the repossession of supernatural finances to rebuild every broken place.
- I decree and declare the repossession and retrieval of blessings thirty, sixty, and a hundredfold.
- I decree and declare the repossession of my career, health, marriage, children, mind, finances, ministry, life and _____.
- I decree and declare the occupation of the land the Lord intends for me.
- I decree and declare constant giving, resulting in a continual influx of blessings - money, deals, things, and time. This is my constant reality.
- I walk in love, joy, peace, patience, kindness, goodness, faithfulness, gentleness, and self-control every moment of the day.
- I walk by faith, and not by not fear, every moment of the day.
- I walk in forgiveness every moment of the day.
- I walk in the full restoration of my life every day.
- I praise and thank God constantly throughout the day.
- I speak in tongues continually throughout the day.
- I engage in constant conversation with God throughout the day.

The playing field levels for me, ensuring sure footing. Unlocking occurs in my life. I decree my eyes open, casting down pride which destroys the adversaries that obscured my inheritance and sonship. I acknowledge it, casting it down. I am a miracle worker, gaining access to ideas that multiply. Destruction will not rule. I overcome any challenges and quench all the fiery darts of the evil one (Eph. 6:16).

The hundredfold return is active in my life in Jesus' mighty Name!

Day 3 — Miracle Mornings

Call upon Him:

Daily, I call upon Him amidst my comings and goings. In the rhythm of life, I remember Him, crying out for His presence. This is how His Name manifests in me. (Read Ps. 88.)

Love:

Daily, I extend love. God is love, and His love is meant to be shared daily with those in close relationships and those around me. I commit to finding ways to express love daily, anticipating the transformative impact that it will have on my life. (Read Deut. 4:1-40, Eph. 5.)

Authority:

Daily, I submit myself to His authority, recognizing the necessity of aligning with God's divine order. I commit to understanding and operating in daily subjection to His authority, and I also pray for those in authority, like governments, police, employers, etc. This practice ensures proper alignment in my life. (Read Luke 7).

Seek Him:

Daily, I seek first the Kingdom of God, His government here on earth, aiming to understand its culture, communication, and governing structure. I commit to walking in God's culture, communicating from a heavenly perspective, and embracing the dynamics of His Kingdom. (Read Matt. 6:33; 1 John 2:3.)

Praise Him:

Daily - moment by moment - I engage in praise, recognizing its power to open the way for the Lord and to add blessings to my life. Praise is the pathway to unlock multiplication, and I commit to praising to see daily transformation and multiplication. (Read Acts 2:47).

In the Name of Jesus, I lift these declarations up before You!

Day 3

MIRACLE MORNINGS

Almighty God, I humbly beseech You to show me any fear that is in me, hindering my pathway through life. Grant me the strength to break free from its shackles, for I accept only the fear from You as a wake-up call as You guide and direct me to Your profound truths. If I carry fear in my heart, I confess it before You, acknowledging my wavering faith, instead of trusting in You completely. Forgive my trespasses, and show me how to confront and overcome fear, so that I am free to walk in Your love for me. Lord, teach me to trust You and live by faith in Your Word.

I know that You shall never put a spirit of fear upon me, for it does not come from You. I thank You instead for the boundless amount of Your unconditional and perfect love, which destroys all fear, according to the teachings of 1 John 4:18. Grant me the power to embrace Your love fully and unconditionally, and to radiate all these love-filled words towards others. I have access to Your divine power through Holy Spirit, my helper and He empowers me to lead the life You have made for me. Teach me, Lord, to assert dominion over my mind, gifted by Your grace, anointed with Your Words, not my fears, so that I may stand strong against the snares of fearful thinking. May I never yield to irrational fear, preventing it from infiltrating my thoughts and life.

Lord, instill within me the ability to sense when fear is approaching. Grant me the skills to boldly declare Your truths when confronted with fear, drawing strength and peace from Your Words of wisdom. You have come as a radiant light into this world, to destroy the works of the evil one, as written in John 12:46.

Fill my heart with Your love and unwavering truth, enabling me to speak out and share Your wisdom to others with unyielding conviction. Teach me the art of unceasing prayer, as written in 1 Thessalonians 5:17. I will not fear the darkness of the night or the fiery arrows of the day, for You have adorned me with the shield of Your salvation and guide me with gentleness. Whenever fear encroaches, I shall put my trust in You, as declared in the Psalms 18:35; 56:3; 91:5).

Day 4 — Miracle Mornings

I decree and declare that:

- Wisdom fills me, allowing me to create and steward wealth wisely.

- God empowers me to make wealth daily, confirming His covenant of blessing, salvation, and deliverance.

- Seeking first the Kingdom, all things pertaining to my life are added unto me.

- I have one Master, choosing God over riches, and as a result, riches are added to me.

- The blessing of the Lord enriches me without sorrow.

- My financial seeds are blest, yielding a great harvest.

- Every seed sown is replenished unto increase.

Lord, You are a miracle-working God and the God of breakthrough. I lift my hands and pray for deliverance, breakthrough, miracles, signs, and wonders. Thank You for overcoming every attack, defeating every assignment of the enemy. I remain consistent in prayer, refusing to quit until revival, glory, and breakthrough come. Every negative and demonic assignment against my life and my family's lives is defeated in the Name of Jesus. Let Your presence and glory be upon us, Oh God, doing something new and fresh. I believe in Your miraculous power and step into a new season of blessings.

I am ready to move into a new place, to cross over into uncharted territories, to inherit new blessings. Lord, I am prepared for restoration and to possess everything stolen from me. By faith, I enter a new season of abundance, health, visions, new commissions and anointings, prophetic dreams and favour. I declare victory and possession of supernatural blessings in every area of my life. I step into the realm of the thousand, return to the realm of the unlimited, the Spirit of the blessing of God. Thank You, Lord, for Your faithfulness.

Day   MIRACLE MORNINGS   4

Confession of the Blood of Jesus

In this Holy and sacred time of confession, I humble myself before You, Father, acknowledging You as my Lord and myself as Your anointed child. It is with a heart of faith that I thank You for Your presence. Today, I lay bare my soul by confessing the Blood of Jesus over my life.

I extend this plea beyond myself to include my family, our homes, vehicles, health, jobs, and finances in the protection of the Blood of Jesus. I cover the very essence of our being - our bodies, minds, wills, emotions, and spirits - with the Blood of the Lamb of God.

As I speak, I stand firm against all diseases, viruses, pestilences, or illnesses that would attack my family or myself. Through the spoken Word, I release Jesus Christ's healing virtue into the very fabric of our bodies, souls, and spirits, trusting in You to heal and restore.

Gratitude fills my heart as I contemplate the miracle of the power of the Blood of Jesus. I recognize myself as one set apart (Holy) and anointed by You, standing firm in our covenant. I assert my right to cast aside every demonic assignment threatening the health and protection of myself and my family.

I declare, with unshakable conviction, that Jehovah-Rophe, the Lord our Healer, has healed us. I anchor my faith in the promise that He keeps us in perfect health all the days of our lives. Furthermore, as I plead the Blood of Jesus, I erect a spiritual barricade against calamities, catastrophes, and hidden dangers that may attempt to infiltrate the sanctuary of my family's life. This confession stands as a testament to my unwavering trust in You Oh Lord, a shield against the evil one that wants to steal, kill and destroy my family and I.

The Blood of Jesus is more than a symbolic gesture; it is the living, pulsating essence of my faith, a testament to Your boundless love and unyielding protection. Thank You Jesus, for just being You!

Day 5: Miracle Mornings

Oh, Father, in heaven, I stand in awe of Your unchanging faithfulness, a beacon that guides the dreams sown in my heart. Grant me a heart unwavering, steadfast on the path of Your light so that I am not swaying to the right or to the left. Lord, anchor my focus on Your perfect will, day by day.

I declare a restoration of Your original intent for my life, and compensation for every loss. I prophesy the recovery of time, the return of stolen blessings, and a miraculous repayment at least seven times. I acknowledge that Jesus is the breakthrough God, prosperity is Your will, and my faith is used as the currency of heaven.

I acknowledge You, God, as deserving of my first and best. I sow seeds with confidence, knowing I will harvest abundantly.

Each day, I am becoming better and more successful. Pride leaves me, making room for the bountiful grace of God. I cast my cares upon You Lord, for Your caring embrace sustains me. Success and prosperity come to me now. I am a positive person. Wealth and wisdom flow into my life effortlessly. Confidence fills me, a divine gift from You Oh Lord. I attract people, finances, and situations that align with my purpose. God's power guides me through every obstacle. I am gifted, wise, and anointed. Wealth manifests in every aspect of my being. Pleasant is my personality, bearing the nine fruits of the spirit. My thoughts and words align with God's divine plan. I am liberated from the snares of the enemy. My vision is clear, and its manifestation is assured.

I declare heaven's agreement with my health and financial needs, invoking the release of divine healing and abundant supply. Thy Kingdom come, Thy will be done!

I decree with authority, and it shall be established unto me.

In the Name of Jesus, I am honoured by my Father, cherished and special. I am the object of His affection, and His love protects me from separation. The Lord favours me, and nothing can sever me from His love.

Day 5

MIRACLE MORNINGS

Redeeming Your Timeline - An Intimate Communion

Oh, Lord, You intimately know me, reading the pages of my heart like an open book. Every word I am about to utter, You've known before I even speak it. You plan my future with kindness, preparing the way and shielding me from the enemy's harm.

Jesus, I am grateful for the redemption of my family and me. You hold the end from the beginning, and I trust in Your sovereignty. I ask You to look at my timeline, redeeming every moment. I apply the precious Blood of Jesus, declaring a new beginning over my life this day. Redemption, restoration, and restitution flow into me now as I break the chains of unforgiveness, curses, and iniquities. I forgive others and myself, asking You to cut out any bitter roots.

Just as time stood still for Joshua and reversed for Hezekiah, I implore You, Father, to work all things in my past for the good of my present and future (Rom. 8:28). Return the years devoured by locusts (Joel 2:25), granting victory in places of defeat and accelerating my purpose to glorify You. Holy Spirit, teach me to number my days, granting me a heart of wisdom (Ps. 90:12). May I weep when it's time and laugh when it's time, marked upright for a peaceful end (Ecc. 3:4; Ps. 37:37). In the mighty Name of Jesus Christ, I pray. Amen.

Reflecting on the Divine Design

"The sons of Issachar had understanding of the times, to know what Israel should do" (1 Chron. 12:32).

"Where could I go from Your Spirit? Where could I run and hide from Your face? Wherever I go, Your hand will guide me; Your strength will empower me" (Ps. 139:7-10).

"To everything, there is a season, a time for every purpose under heaven" (Ecc. 3:1).

Day 6 — Miracle Mornings

I decree and declare.

- I declare protection and diversion of all adversities, attacks, accidents, or tragedies for my family and I through the Blood of Jesus.
- I declare calmness and peace upon every aspect of my life - spirit, soul, and body.
- I declare fear, stress, lack, and other obstacles to be uprooted and rendered harmless in Jesus' Name.
- I declare blessings and abundant goodness for this day, anticipating Holy Spirit's work beyond imagination.
- I choose love, humility, and forgiveness, avoiding judgement, strife, and resentment towards others.
- I declare personal empowerment and purity in all areas of my life.
- I declare the breaking of self-imposed limitations and the possession of new authority.
- I declare the activation of creative abilities, healing, discernment, and prophecy.
- I declare the defeat of enemy manifestations and restoration of my fortunes.
- I declare continuous breakthroughs in all life domains.
- I declare a blossoming, joyfully, with a new voice.
- I declare confusion to depart.
- I declare bondages are broken, prophecies fulfilled, debts of love fulfilled, and abundant blessings received in health, finances, and intellect.
- I live by faith, unaffected by circumstances, abiding in God and His Word, responding in love, releasing faith-filled words.
- I possess prosperity, wisdom, and fruitfulness as I walk in God's light, love, and forgiveness.
- I surrender to God's guidance. I deny myself, allowing God's leading, hearing His voice, prophesying as directed, and submitting all aspects of life to His Spirit.

"God has begun a good work in me, and He is well able to bring it to full completion" (Phil. 1:6).

Day 6

MIRACLE MORNINGS

Lord, grant me the strength to turn away from the allure of temptation, and may my mind be a sanctuary in Your presence. I cast down the imaginations, thoughts, desires of my own soul, putting them at Your feet. In the Name of Jesus, I silence the deceptive whispers of the enemy, choosing to listen only to Your voice. Fill me anew with the precious essence of Holy Spirit, that I may hear You amidst the noise of the world.

With a contrite heart, I seek Your forgiveness for harbouring unforgiveness toward my family and others. Release in me, Oh Lord, the chains of resentment from my heart as I choose to forgive, not only them but also myself. Let this act of mercy bring honour and glory to Your Name, through the Blood of Jesus Christ.

I find peace in the knowledge that I am progressing toward freedom. Every day, I'm getting better at walking with You through the pathways of life. Though my mistakes marred yesterday, I stand before You, seeking Your forgiveness and guidance, and refreshment, knowing that Holy Spirit is with me, and that today is a new day, the day that the Lord has made! (Ps. 118:24) Your love, Lord, is my anchor, and I am grateful for the fresh mercies that embrace me every day.

I reject discouragement and condemnation, for Your Word assures me of Your unwavering love. Jesus, the embodiment of Your love was sacrificed for me, and I am eternally grateful. Today is going to be a great day! Empower me to choose thoughts aligned with Your truth and speak words that resonate with Your wisdom, and not mine. In the Name of Jesus, I declare all of this, trusting in Your grace.

O Heavenly Father, I humbly ask for Your forgiveness and for You to cleanse my soul of sin. Holy Spirit reveal to me any unconfessed sin that may block my relationship with You. I lay bare my heart, acknowledging and confessing the sins of my flesh that I have committed by thoughts, words, and deeds against You, including moments where I failed to love others as You have instructed. I repent and ask for Your mercy.

Day 7 — Miracle Mornings

Ps. 72:7 I am the righteousness of God, and I am flourishing. I have abounding prosperity until the moon is no more.

Ps. 84:11 No good thing will He withhold from me whose walk is upright.

Ps. 112:1-3 Blest am I who fears the Lord, who delights greatly in His commandments. Wealth and riches shall be in my house.

Ps. 128:1-2 I fear the Lord and walk in His ways. I eat the fruit of my labour. Blessings and prosperity are mine.

Ps. 145:16 You open Your hand Lord and satisfy the desire of every living thing.

Ps. 145:19 Lord God, You fulfill my desires, for I fear You.

Prov. 10:22 I have received the blessing of the Lord that has brought me wealth, and He adds no sorrow to it.

Prov. 8:17 - 21 I seek the Lord early and find Him. Riches and honour are with the Lord; yes, durable riches and righteousness that He may cause me, to inherit substance; and He will fill my treasures.

Prov. 10:24 My desires will be granted for I am righteous.

Prov. 11:25 I am a generous person. I will prosper.

Prov. 13:4 I am diligent, and my desires are fully satisfied.

Prov. 13:12 When my desire is fulfilled, it is a tree of life to me.

Prov. 13:21 I have received the righteousness of Christ. Prosperity is my reward.

3 John 2 I prosper in all things, even health, just as my soul prospers.

Day   MIRACLE MORNINGS   7

Prov. 21:21 I have pursued righteousness and love. I have found life, prosperity and honour.

Prov. 22:4 I have received the humility of Christ and the fear of the Lord has brought me wealth and honour and life.

Ecc. 5:19 God, You have given me wealth and possessions and enabled me to enjoy them, to accept my lot and be happy at my work - this is a gift from You.

Mal. 3:10-11 I bring You the whole tithe into the storehouse that there is food in Your house. You, Lord Almighty, have thrown open the floodgates of heaven and poured out so many blessings that I do not have enough room for them. Lord, You rebuke the devourer for my sake so that he will not destroy the fruit of my ground, nor shall the vine fail to bear fruit for me in the field, says the Lord of hosts.

Prov. 103:5 God, You satisfy my desires with good things so that my youth is renewed like the eagles.

Matt. 6:23 I seek first the expansion of God's Kingdom worldwide and all these things shall be added unto me.

2 Cor. 1:20 I am blest going in and blest going out.

John 10:10 Jesus came that I may have life and that I may have it more abundantly.

Eph. 1:3 God has blest me in the heavenly realms with every spiritual blessing in Christ.

Eph. 3:20 Now to You, God who can do exceedingly abundantly above all that I ask or think, according to the power that works in me.

Phil. 4:19 And my God shall supply all my needs according to His riches in glory by Christ Jesus.

Day 8 — Miracle Mornings

- My tithe unto God opens the heavens for me and pours out blessings.

- Because I give God my first and my best in all things, He rebukes the devourer on my behalf.

- Lord, let miracles, signs and wonders, healing, deliverance, and other manifestations of Your glory arise.

- I am extremely fruitful and successful because I abide in Christ.

- Nothing can hinder my fruitfulness and increase because Christ anchors me in sustained blessing.

- Promotions, gifts and God-directed opportunities come to me regularly.

- I am filled with praise and thanksgiving; therefore, breakthroughs constantly manifest in my finances.

- Whatever must die in my life to position me to receive this anointing, let it die, Lord.

- Something great is about to happen in my life. Something new is about to happen. I will not settle for anything less. I confess a thousandfold blessing to come upon my life.

- Lord, You do unusual things. I pray that You will do the unusual in my life.

- Let the earth be full of Your glory Lord. Let my nation, city, and church be full of Your glory. Let my family encounter Your glory.

- God, I pray that You will bless me and multiply me. Release Your grace, favour, peace, and prosperity on my life and my family's lives. God bless my finances by a thousand. Bless my gold and silver, my church, my ministry and my family by a thousand. Let the multiplication anointing come upon my life.

Day 8 — MIRACLE MORNINGS

Oh Father in heaven, Your Word says that I am the head and not the tail, as declared in Deut. 28:13. My journey is one of growing favour with both God and humanity. The hand of the Lord rests upon my life. In the spirit of Caleb, I possess a different and wholehearted devotion, leading to the inheritance of the promised land for myself and my descendants (Num. 14:24).

I am destined to be an owner, free of burdensome debt, not just a tenant. Land, properties, buildings, assets, and inheritances are within my grasp. Through faithfulness in the little, I am entrusted with the much that God bestows upon me, aligning with Luke 16:10.

In every part of my life (spirit, soul, and body) I am destined for health and wholeness. Covered by the Blood of Jesus, I actively participate in the divine communion of His Body and Blood, finding power and strength in Him.

Sickness, infirmity, and disease are far from my family and I. Every cell, bone, tissue, and molecule is renewed in the powerful Name of Jesus. I listen to the voice of the Lord and He protects me from the plagues that befell the Egyptians, for the Lord is my healer (Ex. 15:26).

As the lender and not the borrower, El Shaddai bestows me with abundance. Generously giving and lending to the poor and those around me, I serve as a conduit pipe for the Kingdom of God, as outlined in Deut. 28:12.

The salvation of my entire family is a divine promise. Prodigals return, the backslidden repent, and the lost are found. Following Jos. 24:15 and Acts 16:31, my family is devoted to the Lord.

All my endeavours are destined to prosper, for I commit them unto the Lord (Prov. 16:3). The Spirit of multiplication flows through my actions, and goodness, abundance, and mercy accompany me always (Ps. 23:6).

Lord, I am a willing vessel. Let me carry Your glory to the ends of the earth. Let Your glory be evident in every area of my life.

www.newstartministries.ca

Day 9 — Miracle Mornings

I walk as a living sign and wonder on this earth, dwelling in a realm of continual, sudden God-surprises, signs, wonders, and miracles. Living in the supernatural is His divine will for my life, and I overflow with God's miracles (Is. 8:18).

The Lord of Hosts and the Hosts of Heaven surround me. Angels encircle me, and the glory of the Lord serves as my rear guard (Ps. 91). Protected and watched over by Angels, my loved ones and my belongings are secure.

The Spiritual Gifts You gave me are activated, matured, and effective in the powerful Name of Jesus. Equipped by the grace of the Lord, I stand as a deadly weapon and instrument of righteousness.

Lord, I thank You for seasons of testing, trial, and hardship to purify me and prove me to be a worthy glory carrier.

Life and circumstances must change because I am here. When I open my mouth, something is going to change. When I decree, something is going to change. When I prophesy, something is going to change. When I say new things, something is going to change. My finances are going to change. My family is going to change. My situation is going to change. My career is going to change. My health is going to change. Why? Because greater is He that is in me, than he that is in the world (1 John 4:4).

I declare that I am a son of the Most High God and that Jesus Christ is the source for my finances. I command these finances to come into alignment with the perfect will and purposes of Jesus Christ, Holy Spirit and Father God, Elohim.

I declare: *"For my God shall supply all my needs according to His riches in glory"* (Phil. 4:19).

In my commitment to You Oh God, there exists a profound unity a bond that threads through every person. It is the act of surrendering one's entire being - past, present, and future - into the hands of God, allowing His divine will to unfold as He deems fit.

Day 9 — Miracle Mornings

The remedy of my soul's heartaches and sorrow lies in my ability to accept the burdens of the past. True peace resides not in forgetfulness, nor in mere resignation or worldly distractions. His will, pure and perfect, calls for acceptance, not just resigning to the fact that I suffer from hurts and pain. Instead, I declare, "I trust my fate to the love of God. With open arms and an understanding heart, I welcome what He has permitted to unfold. Knowing that He orchestrates all things for the greater good, I consent to the present with optimism for the future."

I humbly lay my burdens and sorrows at the feet of God. "Lord, you've revealed that vengeance belongs to You alone. You've asked for my forgiveness, and though I've tried repeatedly, the bitterness persists. Now, I offer this resentment to You. Here it is, in my open hand. I pledge not to close my fist and reclaim it. Take charge of these overwhelming emotions, for I trust in Your divine handling."

To trust in God, I must study His nature and His sacred Word. Faith blossoms through hearing and understanding His Word. Faith matures through personal exercise as I apply it to every facet of my life and my families lives.

True faith is rooted in the present, not in vague hopes for the future. It is a living force that shapes our current reality. Absolute honesty is the cornerstone of faith; it cannot coexist with a burdened conscience.

God is saying to me, "You are not alone, for I am by your side. Fear not, abide in Me, and cling to My Word. My promises shall be fulfilled, and your prayers shall find their way to My divine ears. I remain your unwavering source, ensuring your victory. Lift your head high, for the adversary shall not prevail. Rejoice in Me without ceasing, for this is still your year of supernatural increase."

Behold, I decree and prophesy the dawn of a new era, where blessings pour over me without bounds. In the Name of Jesus, I step into the realm of constant favour and prosperity, where every need is met abundantly.

Day   MIRACLE MORNINGS   10

In the radiance of God's love, my spirit soars amidst the trials of life. With unwavering conviction, I stand resolute, fortified by the presence of our Jesus, my personal saviour who is the King of Kings and Lord of Lords. The storms and challenges of life, like waves against the shore, crash upon me, yet I remain unshaken, for my trust rests solely in the hands of God the Father and creator of the universe. In His boundless grace, I witness His benevolent hand guiding me through every temptation, reaffirming my faith and strength in Jesus.

Oh, Heavenly Father, I proclaim liberation from the chains of poverty and discord in Your Name. My barns will overflow with abundance, a testament to Your wonderful grace. No longer shall the deceitful whispers of the evil one cloud my vision, for I am a vessel of Your divine prosperity. With a generous heart, I dedicate my wealth to advancing Your Kingdom. By Your side, I walk with certainty, for Christ's strength dwells within me, empowering me to conquer every obstacle.

Aligned with Holy Spirit, I surrender my life and the lives of my loved ones to Your divine will. May Your purpose reign supreme in our lives, as we bask in the protection of Your mighty hand. With every breath I take, I release the adversary's grip, invoking the precious Blood of Jesus to safeguard our health, relationships, careers, education, and finances. Glory be to Your Name, now and forevermore!

In the fertile soil of faith, I sow seeds of abundance, anticipating a bountiful harvest. Guided by Holy Spirit, I navigate the path of financial triumphs and victories. With a heart overflowing with gratitude, I acknowledge Your boundless provision, as You generously supply the seeds for me to sow.

Empowered by Jesus's grace, I transcend the shackles of lack and poverty. As a cheerful giver, I embrace the joy of giving, knowing that Your love abounds for those who give willingly.

With boldness bestowed by Your grace, I reclaim my life, my family, my city, and my nation from the clutches of the evil one. I declare victory over the whispers of the adversary, for my prayers are mighty and efficacious.

Day 10

MIRACLE MORNINGS

Behold, the gates to financial abundance swing wide open, ushering prosperity into my life. In reverence, I thank You, Lord, for bestowing upon Your people dominion over the earth. With Your anointing, I am equipped with the authority to combat the forces of darkness.

In fervent prayer, I dismantle strongholds and command mountains to yield to Your authority. I commit to standing as a beacon of transformation in this world, declaring, "Enough is enough. The adversary shall not prevail." As it is written, God will bless those who bless me and curse those who curse me (Gen. 12:3). Thus, I march forward, clothed in the armour of faith, for victory is assured in Your Name. Amen.

In this spiritual battle, my weapons are not of this world but are mighty through God for the pulling down of strongholds (2 Cor. 10:4). I stand firm, clothed in the armour of God - faith, righteousness, truth, peace, salvation, and the Spirit's sword, the Word of God - my soul ablaze with His love. For in Him, I am more than a conqueror, an heir of His victory, and a vessel of His grace. We wrestle not against flesh and blood, but against principalities, powers, the rulers of darkness, and spiritual hosts of wickedness in heavenly places (Eph. 6:11-12).

As warriors of light, I cast down the fortresses of doubt, fear, and unbelief. I shatter these illusions that seek to exalt themselves above the knowledge of God. I take captive every rebellious thought, every wandering imagination, and every haughty notion, bringing them into humble submission to the will of Christ (2 Cor. 10:5).

When God seems distant amid discouragement and despair, I know that He is unchanging. While I can't understand His ways or purposes, He is still working in me to bring healing, goodness, and kindness to me.

While I can sin, I declare by the Blood of the Lamb against those who call good evil, and evil good. Guard me, Jesus, from every scheme against righteousness and from those who twist truth into lies to accomplish their evil intentions. Angels protect me from fear and fight against dark, spiritual forces I cannot see. Help me cast down the enemy's thoughts.

Day 11 — Miracle Mornings

Gen. 12:3	I am a blessing to all the peoples of the earth.
Gen. 15:1	Lord, I am not afraid, for You are my shield and my very great reward.
Gen. 18:18	I have received all the blessings of Abraham in Christ. I will surely become a great and powerful nation and all nations on earth will be blest through me.
Gen. 24:35	The Lord has blest me abundantly, and I have become wealthy.
Gen. 26:12	I planted seed, and the same year reaped a hundredfold because the Lord has blest me.
Deut. 7:13	You love me, Lord; You bless me and increase me.
Deut. 8:18	Thank You God for You have given me the ability to produce wealth, and so confirm Your covenant which You swore to my forefathers.
Deut. 11:1	Thank You, God, for increasing me a thousand times and blessing me as You have promised.
Deut. 28:2	The blessings come upon me and overtake me.
Deut. 28:4	All my possessions are blest.
Deut. 28:6	I am blest when I go in and blest when I come out.
Deut. 28:7	The Lord will grant that the enemies who rise up against me are defeated before me. The enemy comes in one direction and flees from me in seven directions.
Deut. 28:8	The Lord sends blessings on everything I put my hand to. The Lord blesses me in the land He has given me.
Deut. 28:11	The Lord has granted me abundant prosperity.
Deut. 28:12	The Lord has opened the heavens, the storehouse of His bounty, to bless all the work of my hands.
Deut. 28:13	The Lord has made me the head and not the tail. I am always at the top and never at the bottom.
Deut. 29:9	I keep the Words of this covenant that I may prosper in all that I do.
Ps. 1:2-3	My delight is in the law of the Lord. On Your law, I meditate day and night. I am like a tree planted by rivers of water which yields its fruit in season and whose leaf does not wither. Whatever I do prospers.

Day 11 — Miracle Mornings

Ps. 21:2-3   You have given me my heart's desire, and have not withheld the request of my lips. For You meet me with the blessings of goodness; You set a crown of pure gold upon my head.

Ps. 25:13   I spend my days in prosperity and my descendants will inherit the land.

Ps. 28:20   I am a faithful person and abound with blessings.

Ps. 34:9   I fear the Lord and lack nothing.

Ps. 35:27   For the Lord has pleasure in my prosperity.

Ps. 37:4   I delight myself in You, Lord, and You give me the desires of my heart.

Ps. 68:19   Blest is the Lord who daily loads me with benefits.

Getting More of Holy Spirit

1. Ask
2. Spend time with God
3. Know the Word
4. Live a Holy (set apart) life
5. Witness
6. Seek honour from God, not people
7. Esteem the fruit

The Fruit

1. Love - spontaneity and an act of your will
2. Joy - is internal; happiness is external - ie. things that make us happy
3. Peace - calm inside, regardless of what is happening
4. Patience - endure pain, delay or trouble without getting angry or upset
5. Kindness - doctrine will not win them but kindness will
6. Goodness - just be a decent person
7. Faithfulness - loyal, integrity, trustworthy
8. Gentleness - don't be provoked
9. Self-control - master your passions and desires

Day 12 — Miracle Mornings

In the Name of Jesus, I bind and cast down the works of the enemy - deception, theft, death, destruction, murder, poverty, injustice, and anything obstructing the flow of God's glory in the earth and particularly in my life and my family.

I submit myself to my elders, walking in humility, knowing that God bestows His grace upon me in this position (1 Peter 5:5).

I command every negative mountain in my life, to be uprooted and cast into the sea. I prophesy to the mountains, declaring them to listen to the Word of the Lord and be removed (Mark 11:23; Ezek. 36:4).

Humbling myself under the mighty hand of God, I anticipate His exaltation in due time (1 Peter 5:6).

O Lord, as You instructed me to, I humble myself, pray, seek Your face, and turn from my wicked ways. You said that if I did You would hear from heaven, forgive my sins, and bring healing to my land. I obediently follow Your command (2 Chron. 7:14).

Lord, help me this day to have a quiet and restful mind, ever conscious of hearing from You. *"You will guard him and keep him in perfect and constant peace whose mind is stayed on You, because he commits himself to You, leans on You, and hopes confidently in You"* (Is. 26:3).

Help me, Lord, not to speak ill of anyone this day and to have good thoughts and words about every situation. Remind me, Lord, to respond in love.

Thank You Jesus that You love me so much that it is not Your will that I endure pain, hardship or strife of any kind.

I am a sacred dwelling, a living sanctuary for the Divine Spirit. 1 Cor. 6:19 says I am assured that Holy Spirit resides within me; a constant and unwavering presence. I walk not alone, for God's Spirit will live forever within me, and the promise of Jesus echoes that *"I will, never leave you nor forsake you."*

Day 12: Miracle Mornings

Daily, I am filled with Holy Spirit, so when I lay hands on the sick, they recover. I hold authority over the dominion of darkness, as declared in Luke 10:19: *"I have given you authority to tread on serpents and scorpions, and over all the power of the enemy,"* so casting out a demon is easy for me.

Since I am a spiritual warrior clad in the armour of God, and called by Him, I stand firm against the wiles of the evil one. The shield of faith, the helmet of salvation, and the sword of the Spirit are my divine property. In the face of adversity, I declare my strength in the Lord, drawing power, wisdom and comfort from Holy Spirit who empowers me.

The peace of God covers me; an unshakeable serenity that shields me from worry, fear, and anxiety. As Phil. 4:7 reveals, the peace of God stands guard over my heart and mind in Christ Jesus. Fear shall not prevail, for Ps. 118 assures me, *"The Lord is for me; I will not fear."*

I hear the still small voice of Holy Spirit, the guiding light, leading me through life's intricate paths. The promise of Ps. 32:8 resonates within me: *"I will instruct you and teach you in the way which you should go."* God's guidance illuminates my steps, offering wisdom and guiding me toward righteous choices.

The joy of the Lord covers all circumstances. In times of despair, Neh. 8:10 echoes, *"The joy of the Lord is your strength."* Through trials, I cling to the assurance of Ps. 30:5, *"Weeping may last for the night, but a shout of joy comes in the morning."*

An ambassador for Christ, I reconcile others to the divine grace of Jesus. As 2 Cor. 5:20 attests, I am an ambassador, and according to 2 Cor. 3:6, an adequate minister of the New Covenant. My qualification lies not in my abilities but in the power of Jesus bestowed upon me.

I bear a purpose and plans for my life are unique to me and sacred. Eph. 2:10 reveals, *"I am God's workmanship,"* a masterpiece fashioned for divine assignments that glorify the Heavenly Father. I am on a sacred mission, destined to fulfill God's purpose for my existence.

Day 13 — Miracle Mornings

Blest am I, seen and cared for by the Father. A provider of my daily needs, as affirmed by Luke 6:38, where giving brings abundance. I shall experience supernatural provision for Phil. 4:19 declares, *"My God supplies all of my need according to His riches in glory by Christ Jesus."*

As a disciple growing daily, my stability deepens, anchored in Jesus's unwavering foundation. In moments of weakness, confusion, or torment, I seek refuge and stability in Christ, as Col. 2:7 proclaims: *"firmly rooted, built up, and established in my faith."* Strong roots in Christ yield abundant fruit.

Accessing His grace that never fails, I find strength in every trial through Jesus. The promise of 2 Cor. 12:9 resonates within me, *"My grace is sufficient for you, for power is perfected in weakness."* Sufficient strength for each day flows from the endless well of God's grace.

I am destined to live eternally with Christ. Rom. 6:23 declares, *"The free gift of God is eternal life in Christ Jesus our Lord."* My faith in Jesus secures a place in the Lamb's Book of Life, ensuring my place in the heavenly city when this earthly journey concludes.

Covered in eternal love, Jer. 31:3b declares, *"I have loved you with an everlasting love; I have drawn you with unfailing kindness."* God's love, beyond comprehension, extends beyond my shortcomings and sins, embracing me with kindness and mercy.

My Father delights in me as a beloved son/daughter, a cherished child of God. Eph. 1:6 affirms, *"He made us accepted in the beloved,"* extending a warm welcome in my Father's house.

Embracing the sacred journey of my life, today, I joyfully embrace the divine responsibility for every aspect - the triumphs, the lessons, and the defeats.

Day 13 — Miracle Mornings

I stand firm, choosing not to lay blame on external forces, circumstances beyond my control, or other people. There is no "blame game" in my life. Instead, I commit to pursuing my divinely ordained vision, a plan by God for me to live the radiant life of my (His) dreams. Farewell to yesterday, and a warm embrace to today and the promise of tomorrow!

My life's compass is guided by principles rooted in the Word of God, driven by excellent values, which then are impactful on all society (Is. 58:12).

With clarity, I write down and pray over my purpose and mission, diligently nurturing my gifts, talents, resources, networks, relationships, and opportunities. I am moulding success and manifesting all I was destined to be, do, achieve, and accomplish (Hab. 2:2-3).

Today, I rise, affirming Your wisdom, favour, and grace Lord, to pour over my day (Rom. 12:3-18).

In this new day, where mercy is renewed, and opportunities abound, I declare a day of divine vision, inspiration, wisdom, and boundless hope (Ps. 31:24).

For this day is a masterpiece of God's creation, purposefully designed for my discovery, fulfillment, and manifestation of purpose (Rom. 8:28; 2 Tim. 1:9).

Today, I surrender my will, echoing the prayer, *"Not my will, but Your will be done"* (Matt. 6:10).

I vow not to squander this day in the realm of mediocrity; instead, I shall invest it for good, turning my time into gain, my actions into success, and my path into a legacy free of regrets (Rom. 14:12).

Laughter joyously erupts within me when confronted with falsehoods from the adversary.

Day 14 — MIRACLE MORNINGS

- Today, I willingly follow the divine plans laid out for me (Ps. 37:23).
- In this moment, I cultivate a Tranquility that remains unshaken (Phil. 4:7-11).
- I align my priorities with Holy Spirit, focusing on the essence of the Christian walk of life (Matt. 6:33).

- My journey unfolds under the watchful eye of God, ensuring that only goodness graces my path (Ps. 136:1-3).

- Understanding that enduring success rests on the foundation of truth, authenticity, integrity, justice, and love, I engage in endeavours that uphold these virtues, treating each task as an offering to Jesus (Col. 3:23).

- I dwell in a realm of boundless potential, where every decision made today reshapes the contours of the day and tomorrow as well. With God, all things are possible (Matt. 19:26; 2 Cor. 9:6).

- I navigate life as a visionary, a leader of thoughts (Prov. 29:18; Is. 58:6-14).

- My lifestyle, marked by holiness, becomes a fertile ground for peace, success, and prosperity (Heb. 12:14).

- I decree victory over challenges, drawing strength from God (1 Cor. 15:57; 1 John 5:4).

- I resist the temptation to be slothful, understanding that diligence shall reign (Prov. 12:24).

- I prosper and I am blest where divinity has planted me (Ps. 1:1-3; Deut. 28:3).

- Authority flows through me, resonating with the power of God.

- In the face of daunting challenges, I declare, "Only good can come out of this" (Gen. 50:20; Rom. 8:28).

Day   MIRACLE MORNINGS   14

- With honour, respect, influence, and dignity, I walk down the road of faith (Deut. 28:10).

- My existence knows no bounds, limitations, or covers (1 Chron. 4:10).

- I foster relationships that are mutually enriching and fruitful (Prov. 13:20; Rom. 12:10; Eph. 5:1-2, 21).

- Time and opportunities are treasures I cherish, making the most of each moment (Eph. 5:15-16).

- I replace unhealthy habits with those that nurture my well-being (Rom. 12:1-2).

- In faith, I deepen my connection with God (Heb. 11:1, 6; Mark 11:24).

- I relentlessly pursue improvement and refinement in all facets of my life (Phil. 3:12). I walk in the fullness of Holy Spirit every day.

- My conduct is characterized by honesty and ethical integrity (2 Peter 1:5-7).

- I honour my body with the care it deserves - exercise, rest, and nutrition for it is a temple of Holy Spirit (1 Cor. 6:19-20).

- Witnessing improvements daily, I grow stronger, embracing vibrant health and nurturing my soul (3 John 2).

- Amidst prosperity, health, and beauty, I find my dwelling place (Ps. 16:6).

- I unlock my potential, sowing seeds of spirituality and grace.

- My prayers resonate with the divine and manifest powerful and effective outcomes.

- God abundantly fulfills all my financial needs in alignment with His divine plan.

Day 15 — Miracle Mornings

- In moments of prayer for guidance, breakthroughs, and divine intervention, I focus on gaining strategies for the realization of my vision. These precious moments are opportunities to prepare for the future, refine skills, or extend a helping hand to others.

- I am liberated from the entanglements of sin, embracing a life attuned to God's divine will.

- Each step I take is a journey towards ever-increasing health, guided by my spiritual energy.

- I am covered in a supernatural shield of protection as I navigate the path of life.

- I declare this day blest, stirring the mighty God to manifest exceedingly and abundantly beyond all my expectations. I eagerly anticipate the goodness of God unfolding today.

- I consistently channel divine encounters, sharing the transformative power of God with those around me.

- Through the embrace of Jesus, I am covered in 100% love, rendering me worthy to receive all of God's abundant blessings.

- Every family member is divinely blest and profoundly loved by the grace of Jesus.

- By declaring God's support, I set the unyielding course of my life, immune to defeat, discouragement, depression, or disappointment.

- I am elevated as the head, blest with insight, wisdom, ideas, and divine strategies.

- As I articulate God's promises, they swiftly come to fruition, dismantling all my life's attacks, oppressions, and fears.

- Today, I walk in the wisdom of God, making righteous decisions and speaking words of grace in every circumstance.

Day 15: Miracle Mornings

- Divine appointments await me, filled with the power to heal, prophesy, lead other souls to Christ, minister deliverance, and release signs and wonders.

- Expectation fills my heart for today to be the most spiritually, emotionally, relationally, and financially fulfilling day in Jesus' Name.

- Anchored in a covenant with God through the Blood of Jesus, divine protection and provision overflow over me and my family.

- My Angels faithfully carry out the Word of God, ensuring divine intervention on my behalf.

- Adversities, attacks, accidents, and tragedies destined for me or my family are divinely diverted in Jesus' Name.

- I speak peace to the raging waters in my life, mind, emotions, body, home, and family.

- Every mountain of fear, discouragement, stress, depression, lack, and insufficiency dissolves and is cast into the sea in Jesus' Name.

- I drive out from our midst the spirits of carelessness, laziness, and apathy, invoking a fresh breeze of prayer instead to invigorate the Body of Christ. Let the fires of revival burn brightly in our midst, consuming all that is impure and igniting within us a passion for Thy Holy will.

- Since I am walking in the fullness of Holy Spirit in my life, I know that I am healed, sanctified, blest, anointed, praised, and prosperous by the Blood of the Lamb.

- I know this is in my physical health, my financial well-being, the strength of my relationships, the protection of my home, vehicles and other family assets. In short, "I am blest going in and blest going out!" (Deut. 28:6)

Day   MIRACLE MORNINGS   16

Oh Father God, guide my steps along the path of righteousness, fortifying my spirit against the shadows of fear. I surrender my life, dreams, and fears into Your tender care, for I find refuge and strength in You alone. Let Your loving kindness sing to my soul at the dawn of each day, a gentle reminder of Your unwavering love for me. Illuminate the path of life before me so that I may walk in alignment with Your divine will.

Grant me the strength to turn away from the calls of darkness, to shun all that tarnishes the purity of my walk with You. Teach me how to forgive, so I may release resentment and embrace the freedom of love. Shield me from the allure of temptation, that I may walk sin-free in the light of Your truth.

In the sanctuary of Your grace, reveal unto me how I must course-correct, guiding me to relinquish all that falls short of Your highest purpose for my life. Empower me to witness Your goodness and share Your testimonies with others.

May my life be a living testament to Your boundless grace, love and glory. In the face of fear's relentless assault, may I stand firm, fortified by the unwavering faith that You have instilled within me.

I offer this prayer in Jesus's Name, trusting in Your unfailing love and provision. Amen

Heavenly Father,

With my heart lifted in praise and my spirit ignited by Holy Spirit, I come before Your throne. In the mighty Name of Jesus Christ, I stand firm, declaring victory over every scheme of the enemy. By the authority vested in me through Jesus Christ, I bind and rebuke all forms of division, discord, and strife that seek to hinder my walk with You.

Day 16 — MIRACLE MORNINGS

In the light of Your presence, my family and I cover ourselves with the precious Blood of Jesus, shielding us from every curse and negative word spoken against us. We choose forgiveness over bitterness, blessing those who curse us and releasing divine favour upon those who oppose us. I dismantle the enemy's strongholds, breaking every chain of deception and manipulation.

As a child of the Most High, I walk in the righteousness of Christ, empowered by Holy Spirit. I declare my authority over every demonic force and decree that no weapon shall be formed against my family, and I shall prosper. Clothed in the armour of God, I step into this day with confidence, knowing that Your Spirit guides my every step.

Father, I surrender my life afresh to Your divine purpose. Anoint me for the ministry You have ordained, igniting my heart with Holy passion. I speak forth divine appointments, open doors of opportunity, and God-ordained encounters. Surround me, O Lord, with a hedge of protection, and dispatch Your Angels to guard me and my family in all our ways.

In the Name of Jesus, I pray. Amen.

I embark on this day with a consciousness of divine dependency, allowing the Spirit of God to be in me. I walk in total dependency upon Him because I am conscious that the power in me does not emanate from me, but from Him (Eph. 1:18-20; 1 John 4:4).

I do my part in making this world a better place (Mark 16:15-18; Is. 61:1).

I realize I cannot embrace what You have for me in my future until I let go of my past (Phil. 3:13-14).

I commit my life, my vision, and all my endeavors to You (Ps. 37:5).

And, as a result, I am blest going in and blest going out! (Deut. 28:6)

Day 17 — Miracle Mornings

I refuse to live defeated, discouraged, depressed, or disillusioned. I decree peace is within the walls of my house and within my borders (Ps. 122:7; 147:14).

I choose to face daily with deliberate action based on my faith, values, passion, and vision for making this world a better place (Ps. 25:12).

I choose: (Deut. 30:19)
- life over death
- blessings over curses
- abundance over scarcity
- success over failure
- humility over pride
- serving over being served
- honour over dishonour
- truth over lies
- transparency over deception
- openness over closed-mindedness
- righteous living over unrighteousness
- character over compromise
- trust over distrust
- love over hate
- peace and harmony over conflict and war
- giving over receiving
- faith over disbelief
- courage over fear
- progress over stagnation
- prosperity over poverty
- health over sickness
- kindness over cold heartedness
- generosity over stinginess
- joy over depression
- diligence over laziness
- honesty over dishonesty
- morality over immorality

Day 17 — MIRACLE MORNINGS

I surrender, Lord. With every heartbeat, I release the grip of anxiety, for I trust in the unfolding of divine timing (Phil. 4:6).

I welcome the gentle hands of patience, allowing them to break, mould, and make me, my soul, into completeness, a masterpiece of Your incredible design. In this completeness, I lack nothing, for I am held in the abundance of Your grace (James 1:4).

I lift my spirit to the heavens, elevating my expectations to the realm of the miraculous. I find refuge in the quiet stillness of faith, knowing that all things are possible through You (Ps. 62:5; Eph. 3:20).

My thoughts are of prosperity, where seeds of positivity and success flourish abundantly. With every thought and by speaking Your Words that do not come back to You void, I shape my reality, aligning myself with You (Phil. 4:8; Jos. 1:8-9).

I am a vessel of divine wisdom, a channel for the mind of Christ to flow through me. With clarity of thought and purity of heart, I navigate the cycles of life, guided by Your eternal light of truth and Word (Rom. 12:2; 1 Cor. 2:16).

Before every decision, I seek Your counsel Holy Spirit, trusting in Your wisdom that transcends human understanding. By doing this, I find clarity and direction (Prov. 3:5-6).

I am the architect of my reality, shaping it with the substance of my Spirit-led thoughts and Your spoken Words. Today, I choose to dwell on the beauty of truth, the purity of love, and the radiance of goodness. In this sacred dwelling, I find peace and fulfillment (Phil. 4:8).

Your thoughts toward me are pure and purposeful; all circumstances align for my benefit (Jer. 29:11; Rom. 8:28).

Today, I am imbued with the wisdom of God, guiding my thoughts, words, and decisions towards righteousness.

Day 18

MIRACLE MORNINGS

- I proclaim and affirm that the essence of peace shall dissipate all confusion and tumultuous circumstances in my life.

- I decree and declare the immobilization of all evil forces that bring turmoil, strife, and discord into my life.

- I declare the tranquil serenity within me shall flow forth to soothe the hearts of others who are in some form of tribulation.

- Every shackle of oppression and evil dominion shall be shattered under the power and authority of God's Word.

- By the authority vested in me through Holy Spirit, I decree the annihilation of every diabolical evil scheme aimed at my path.

- The spirit of indebtedness, which sows seeds of anxiety, fear, and weariness, is hereby severed at its roots by the mighty power of the Holy Name of Jesus.

- Every unholy pact, I knowingly or unwittingly entered, now crumbles by the power of the Name of Jesus.

- In moments of trial, Holy Spirit shall pave a path of deliverance, offering solace, refuge and strength to me.

- The grip of regression is shattered, as I stride forward into the realms of advancement and growth.

- Every shattered dream, dormant vision, and extinguished hope that has plagued me is now being revived and reignited.

- God's orchestrated timing is my guide, ensuring I embrace each season without delay or oversight.

- I am being realigned to my destiny in life.

Day   MIRACLE MORNINGS   18

- My tongue is being used as an instrument of praise, resounding with sounds of jubilation and gratitude.

- I am empowered to perform mighty deeds, manifesting the glory of God in every situation that I walk into.

- Through the indwelling strength of Christ, I am endowed with the capacity to overcome all obstacles, and every decree uttered in His Name is fulfilled in Jesus' Name.

- Under God's protection, my family and I find refuge, dwelling in the secret sanctuary of His hands.

- Shielded from the snares and pestilences of the evil one, I stand secure under the watchtower of His guardianship.

- The sanctity of my character and reputation will remain unblemished, upheld by the hand of God's divine vindication.

- I find solace and safety, sheltered from the storms of life.

- May the winds of blessing carry forth the names of myself and my family, ensuring our legacy is etched in the Lamb's Book of Life.

- Every loss shall be redeemed, and the tears sown in anguish shall yield an abundant harvest of joyous sounds.

- My name shall resound with honour, shielded from the arrows of scandal and disgrace.

- Help me discern Your will and determine my times and seasons (1 Chron. 12:32; Ecc. 3:1).

- Let me not covet what belongs to someone else (Ex. 20:17; Rom.13:9).

Day 19 — Miracle Mornings

Lord, I find myself woven intricately into Your design, blest by Your hand; therefore, I am a conduit pipe of blessings unto others. Blessings come to me, and I pour them out to others. Each dawn, as the sun rises, I am reminded to count my blessings, to turn my gaze heavenward, and offer gratitude to You, God, my Father, whose goodness knows no bounds. Your gentle mercies flow over my life, nurturing my soul and ensuring that goodness and grace blossom in abundance.

In the realm of the spirit, I stand adorned with the favour of God, a crown of glory upon my head for all eternity. This favour draws unto me the gifts of blessing and positions me as a lighthouse of influence amidst the turbulence of this world. Even when adversity seeks to cast its shadow upon my path, I stand firm in the assurance that the enemy's advances will crumble before God's mighty hand. For my God is one of breakthrough, who leads me triumphantly, scattering the devil of darkness in seven directions.

As I increase my journey with Holy Spirit, I ascend from glory to glory, each step an ascent towards His crown of glory. Supernatural provision manifests in my life as a testament to His abundant grace and unfailing love. And lo, amidst the trials and tribulations of my life, I am comforted by the knowledge that Angels of breakthrough make way the path for me, lining it with blessing after blessing.

I ask You, Father God, to pour out Your grace, favour, and Your peace upon my family and I. Work wonders in our midst, O God. Reveal Your strength and Your glory in the land of the living. Let every knee bow, and every tongue confess, that Jesus Christ is Lord, the Alpha and the Omega, the Beginning and the End.

I pray for the ministers of the Word, those who are entrusted with the task of shepherding Your flocks. May they be delivered from the shackles of religious dogma and traditional bondage, infused with a righteous indignation against injustice and oppression. May their hearts overflow with love and compassion for the downtrodden and the afflicted, as they wield the sword of truth against the forces of darkness.

Day 19

MIRACLE MORNINGS

- Bless this week and the month that lies ahead of me. Empower me to abound in every good work (2 Cor. 9:8).

- Give me the grace to face my greatest challenge (Rom. 5:20).

- Let me be steadfast, immovable, and unshakable in all things and in all situations (1 Cor. 15:58).

- Thank You, Lord, for preparing and equipping me for the greater works (John 14:12).

- Thank You for the presence of Your Holy Spirit, the greatest empowerment specialist, who enlightens me concerning my future (John 16:13).

- I yield myself to Your guidance (Ps. 73:24).

- I cast my cares upon You because You care for me (1 Peter 5:7).

- Help me govern my time according to Your revealed will for my life (Rom. 8:27).

- Thank You for empowering me and strengthening me to accomplish every goal attached to the divine vision You have given me (Deut. 8:18; 1 Peter 5:10).

- I yield my desires and will to You, Lord. You give me the desires of my heart (Ps. 37:4).

- Summon those people Lord who are divinely appointed to walk alongside and be part of the vision You have given me (2 Chron. 2:1-18).

- With every breath, I enter a place of prayer, hosting Your presence. In this communion, I find strength, guidance, and solace (Eph. 6:18; 1 Thess. 5:17).

Day 20 — Miracle Mornings

Words of Affirmation

Read and pray at least once daily or as often as is needed for issues of rejection.

The truth of God's Word flows through me, for I am one of His chosen; "a thing of beauty," boundless capability, and love. In the eyes of God who made me, I am cherished and precious, a unique creation crafted with tender love and care. When my spirit falters, I seek forgiveness with humility, knowing that divine grace is upon me.

As a beloved child of God the Father, I walk this earthly realm with an open heart, embracing everyone with love, warmth, and compassion. Yesterday's wounds don't affect me because the winds of healing are upon me, and I release hurts and embrace intimacy with Holy Spirit. I forgive! My relationships with others are healed because I am healed, sanctified, blest, anointed, praised and prosperous by the Blood of the Lamb. I walk in honesty, integrity and reverence with Holy Spirit.

The wisdom of the Bible resides within me, igniting the depths of my intellect and creativity. With a mind attuned to the Word, I navigate life's complexities with clarity and resolve, for I am endowed with the consciousness of God and His will.

Diligence and fidelity are my companions on this journey of life, as I tread the path of excellence guided by His divine hand. Every endeavour I undertake flourishes under His watch, for triumph is my birthright in the realm of Christ.

With unwavering faith, I surrender and relinquish control to Holy Spirit. I am a vessel of His will, flowing in unity with Him.

Success is a divine appointment for my family and I. Through Christ, I draw strength to surmount any obstacle, greeting each new day's dawn as a beacon of hope and gratitude.

Day 20

MIRACLE MORNINGS

Each day unfolds with steadfast vision, as directed to me by Holy Spirit.

I am filled with passion and power with each breath, radiating confidence and vitality. The Word of God within me is a wellspring of extra strength and wisdom. It is the core of my life.

Before time began, God made me, loved me unconditionally and wholly accepted me. Every fiber of my being resonates with health, vitality, and divine love, for I am sanctified and blest by the Blood of the Lamb.

In Your divine presence, Father, I declare:

- You, O Lord, are my source of strength, hope, and unwavering shield (Lam. 3:24; Ps. 28:7).

- By Your Spirit, all I achieve is made possible; in Your might, I prevail (Zech. 4:6; Matt. 16:18).

- Your blessings adorn the works of my hands, and Your wisdom enriches my soul (Deut. 28:12; Col. 3:16).

- While the world may falter, I soar on wings of faith; in You, I find renewal and endurance (Is. 40:30-31).

- The Spirit within me testifies I am a cherished child of God, heir to His promises and glory (Rom. 8:16-18).

- Firmly rooted in Christ's freedom, my hope remains unshakable, my future secure (Gal. 5:1; Prov. 23:18).

- Every thought submits to Christ's authority; through Him, I am empowered for all things (2 Cor. 10:5; Phil. 4:13).

- For Yours is the Kingdom, the power, and the eternal glory (Matt. 6:13).

Day 21 — Miracle Mornings

Longevity

I am not a victim of circumstance; instead, I am embedded with purpose and significance. The Word is planted in me; therefore, I shall flourish and bear abundant fruit. Every step I take resonates with the promise of fulfillment of His Word in me, for I am destined to walk with Him.

With each passing day, I embrace the fullness of life, drawing from the wellspring of joy that flows within me. I am attuned to a long and healthy life, for my spirit is fortified by Holy Spirit in me. The schemes of darkness shall not sway the hands of time, for I am a warrior of light, steadfast in my commitment to Jesus, the King of Kings and Lord of Lords. *"With long life I will satisfy him, and show him My salvation"* (Ps. 91:16).

With resolute faith, I declare that my spirit, soul, and body are vessels of power; vessels through which Holy Spirit flows. This world does not define me, but by Him who resides within me. With each passing moment, I shall run the race set before me, with unwavering faith and unyielding determination, and when the final chapter of my story is written, Jesus will be waiting for me and He will declare, *"Well done, good and faithful servant!"* (Matt. 25:23)

I Will Live, I Will Not Die

Chorus
I will live, I will not die,
By the power of God's Word, I'm kept alive,
Until I have run the race, fought the fight, I am satisfied,
I will live, I will not die.

Verse
Until I am old and gray,
He'll sustain me every day,
All of His will I will fulfill,
With every sickness and test, I will prevail,
And God's glory, I will tell,
I will live, I will not die. *

* Apostle Keith Moore recorded this in one of his sermon messages over 30 years ago.

Day 21 — Miracle Mornings

I decree and declare that:

- I am a true worshiper of Jesus, the One who is my breakthrough! I adore Him and constantly exalt Him as the God of breakthrough throughout my day.

- I sow bountifully in confident faith and obedience. Therefore, I reap bountifully with confidence.

- Every seed I sow has a corresponding harvest attached to it.

- I make sound and wise investments of my finances, talent, and time as the Spirit leads.

- I meditate daily and walk in obedience to God's Word; therefore, I am like a tree planted by rivers of living water. My leaves do not wither and I constantly bear fruit and prosper (Ps. 1:3). I live in God's blessed abundance.

- I enjoy everything that leads to life and to godliness. All the great, precious, and magnificent promises in the Word have been granted to me in Jesus. Likewise, every spiritual blessing in the heavenly realms has also been given to me (Eph. 1:3).

- I will not call to my mind the former things or ponder the things of the past. I look to the new things that the Lord will do. They will spring forth even now (Is. 43:18-19).

- I am a new creature in Christ. Old things have passed away and all things have become new (2 Cor. 5:17).

- Lord put within me a new heart and a new spirit and take away my stoney heart and give me a heart of flesh (Ezek. 36:26).

- Let my barns be filled with plenty and my presses burst forth with new wine (Prov. 3:10).

Day 22 — MIRACLE MORNINGS

- Lord, I believe You are the God of the new thing, and I declare today new beginnings. New things will begin to spring forth in my life.

- This is a new season, day, and time and I speak new strength, power, authority, and new joy into my life.

- New visions, dreams, ideas, thoughts, witty inventions, a new mind, and a new way of thinking do I decree into my life (Prov. 8:12).

- In the Name of Jesus, new finances, businesses, properties, prosperity, and new money are coming my way.

- I decree new songs, praise, worship, anointing, breakthroughs, spiritual levels, revelation, understanding, and wisdom. Let them all be released in my life.

- I believe, Father, that as I declare and decree, these new things will begin to manifest today and, in the days, months, and years to come.

- I believe, Father, You will do something new in my life. The old is passing away, and restoration is here now! The new thing is arising. New blessings are being released in my life, in the Name of Jesus.

- With my words and mouth, I decree new things in the Name of Jesus, and I believe, expect and look for new things to be established.

- I overlook the world's inconveniences and the inconsideration of people because I know that whatever is beyond my control is under Your control, for my times are in Your hand (Ps. 31:15).

- I run a very successful _____ (ministry/business/household/career) because You are with me. (Jos. 1:8; Ps. 107:23).

- I leave a legacy for the next generation. Let my days speak and my years teach wisdom (Job 32:7).

Day 22 — Miracle Mornings

- I am diligent in earning and managing money, saving and investing more and spending less (Prov. 6:6; 13:22; Ecc. 11:1-2).

- I am financially independent and live in the realm of success. I receive a substantial return on my investments (Deut. 28:8).

- I live in the realm of abundance. I have more than enough and overflow. My days of barrenness, lack, and struggle are over. My posterity (future generations) and loved ones will never be homeless or beg for bread (Deut. 28:11; Ps. 37:25).

- I stand blameless, clothed in the righteousness of Jesus. Eph. 1:4 says, *"For he chose us in Him before the creation of the world to be holy and blameless in His sight."*

- As a cherished member of His family, the Father longed for my embrace. Rom. 8:15 echoes, *"Received the spirit of adoption... crying out, 'Abba, Father,'"* affirming my bold proclamation of God as my loving "Daddy," securing my place in His embrace.

- United with Christ, my inheritance overflows with heavenly treasures. Rom. 8:17 declares, *"An heir of God"* and a *"fellow heir with Christ,"* ensuring I receive boundless blessings from the Father's hand.

- Freed from chains of sin, I stand firm against temptation. Rom. 6:18 declares, *"A slave of righteousness,"* breaking free from past sins and addictions. In Christ, I am renewed, as 2 Cor. 5:17 proclaims.

- Triumphant in Christ, Rom. 8:37 declares that I am, *"More than a conqueror,"* as Christ's victory on the cross ensures my triumph. I overcome all obstacles with God within me, as 1 John 4:4 declares.

- With the cleansing Blood of Christ, I find forgiveness and purification. Eph. 1:7 assures, *"Redemption through His blood, forgiveness of sins,"* erasing my transgressions from memory.

Day 23 — Miracle Mornings

- Immersed in scripture, I absorb His wisdom, renewing my spirit with each Word (Jos. 1:8).

- As a co-creator with the Father, I shape my destiny, releasing blame and excuses.

- With love and compassion, I serve others, finding my purpose (Luke 22:26; 1 Tim. 5:8).

- Grant me, Father, the grace to fulfill my divine purpose (Ps. 84:11; Heb. 4:16). Engulf me in Your wisdom and understanding (Is. 11:2-3).

- I affirm that *"everyone who calls upon the Name of the Lord shall be saved"* (Rom. 10:13). Therefore, I beseech the Name of Jesus for salvation, healing, and deliverance. O Lord, I summon Your presence to release the fervent prayers of the saints upon the earth. Unleash Your mighty power; let Your divine judgement prevail in the Name of Jesus.

- May those ensnared by the world find liberation from the bonds that entangle them, by the authority of Jesus' Name.

- May the deeds of the unrighteous leaders bring conviction, and if they refuse repentance, may they be displaced from their thrones and offices. Let virtuous leaders emerge to guide with integrity. May Your Kingdom come, Your will be done on earth as it is in heaven!

- Lord, I release Your grace, favour, and peace over Your beloved. Perform miracles, O God; reveal Your omnipotence on our behalf upon this earth.

- Let every knee bow and every tongue confess that Jesus is Lord (Phil. 10:11).

- In Christ, I am a new creation; the old has passed away, behold, the new has come (2 Cor. 5:17).

Day 23: Miracle Mornings

- God, I intercede for preachers yet to delve into the realms of deliverance. May You liberate them from the demons of religious rigidity and tradition. Ignite within them a righteous fervour against injustice and oppression, amplifying their love and compassion for the downtrodden.

- Father, I anticipate the advent of salvation and deliverance upon my nation and wait for a revival to sweep through this nation and Your church.

- I reject the influence of Jezebel and Ahab in my life, invoking the anointing of Jehu to dismantle their grasp. I shall repent and steadfastly hold onto what is true (Rev. 2:20-25).

- I have received the Gift of Holy Spirit through repentance and baptism (Acts 2:38).

- Lord, I repent and turn away from idols and abominations (Ezek. 14:6).

- Lord, I express gratitude for the forthcoming restoration and revival. Enlighten me to discern the aspects of my life that need purification for Your blessings and favour to flow abundantly.

- Lord, may You restore and light my path to deliverance (Ps. 80:19).

- Thank You, Lord, for the restoration of my fortunes (Jer. 49:6; Joel 3:1).

- Heal me, O Lord, lead me, and restore comfort unto me (Is. 57:18).

- I shall not dwell on the past. Instead, I anticipate the new works You will unveil. They shall spring forth even now (Is. 43:18-19).

- Lord, instill within me a new heart and spirit, removing the hardness and granting me tenderness (Ezek. 36:26).

Day 24 — Miracle Mornings

- In Your Name, O Lord, I declare new beginnings. I prophesy new strength, power, authority, and joy into my life. I decree new visions, dreams, ideas, and a renewed mindset. May new opportunities and prosperity flow abundantly.

- Father, as I speak and decree, may these new manifestations spring forth, beginning today and permeating my life in the days, months, and years ahead.

- I believe, Father, that You are orchestrating a new work in my life. The old is fading, the new is emerging, and fresh blessings are unfolding in the Name of Jesus.

- With my words and mouth, I decree newness in Jesus' Name, eagerly awaiting and expecting the establishment of these new realities. In Jesus, I am victorious! His divine hand leads me through each moment, lighting the path of triumph.

- Guided by Holy Spirit, I am inspired by His presence which infuses me with courage and direction, for He is the very essence of my life.

- I am attentive and listening to the gentle whispers of Holy Spirit, finding peace amidst the chaos of this world.

- In God's love, victory encompasses me. His divine essence envelops me, guiding me with perfection. His eternal love sustains me, carrying me through every trial and triumph.

- Step by step, I journey with God the Father, buoyed by His divine love. With each stride, His presence propels me towards greatness.

- I am fortified and His divine strength courses through me, breaking all bonds of darkness.

- Clad in the armour of God, I am shielded by His divine power. I bind myself to the forces of His incarnation, resurrection, and omnipotence.

Day 24 — Miracle Mornings

- I am guided and protected by Angels (Ps. 91:11; Luke 4:10).

- I align myself with the divine wisdom of God, trusting in His guidance and shelter.

- His Words are in my mouth and His hand guides my every step.

- With unwavering faith, I march forward, embraced by the shield of God's love.

- His divine presence is my fortress, and His path leads me to everlasting victory.

Putting on the armour of God, I bind myself today to:

- The power of Christ's incarnation in baptism and the power of His crucifixion at His burial.

- The power of His resurrection and ascension, and the power of His coming on Judgement Day.

- The power of God to guide me, God's might to uphold me, God's wisdom to teach me, God's eye to watch over me, God's ear to hear me, God's Word to give me speech, God's hand to guide me, God's way to lie down before me, God's shield to shelter me.

- A divine transformation flows through my being. No longer shall the shadows of my past ensnare me, for You, Lord God, in Your infinite grace, have washed away the scarlet stains of my sins. You have rewoven the fabric of my existence, rendering it as pure as driven snow (Is. 1:18).

- The gift of redemption bestowed upon me shall not be squandered, for I recognize the sacredness of every moment You grant. Time, a precious currency, is bestowed upon me abundantly, and I vow to honour it with purpose and gratitude.

Day — MIRACLE MORNINGS — 25

- Just as Hannah received a miraculous blessing, so too shall blessings overflow into my life, in the Name of Jesus.

- Through Jesus, an eternal triumph is woven into every aspect of my existence, from the depths of my soul to the breadth of my possessions.

- No earthly weapon, crafted by the hands of doubt or fear, can thwart God's plan for my prosperity.

- Each step I take is bathed in His divine favour and blessings.

- The radiant glow of blessings covers me, drawn by the covenant I share with Jesus.

- Blessings cascade upon me, eager to overtake my journey and illuminate my path.

- In the Name of Jesus, all debts are settled and erased from my life.

- Though the adversary may scoff and scorn, seeking to sow seeds of doubt and shame, today marks the dawn of my breakthrough.

- Today is a day of divine creation, where my spirit's womb is opened wide to birth dreams, visions, and aspirations. In the Name of Jesus, I prophesy their manifestation with the finances in place to carry them out.

- I declare that my essence resonates with favour and grace, woven into the fabric of my being by the divine hand.

- God, in His infinite mercy, lifts me high above the enemy's attacks, shielding me from shame and ridicule.

- I am not bound by curses; blessings liberate me.

- My prayers germinate seeds of extraordinary, heavenly significance.

Day 25 — Miracle Mornings

- With unwavering faith, I proclaim my prosperity and blessings, knowing that God's grace will work wonders in my life.

- In my desperation, I am drawn to the throne of God, where prayers find their fulfillment and miracles unfold.

- I trust in the promise that no weapon formed against me shall prosper (Is. 54:17).

- In my hour of need, God stands as my refuge, my beacon of light, and my fortress (Ps.46:1).

- Oh Lord, hear my desperate plea, as I stretch forth my hands in prayer, yearning for Your divine intervention.

- In the darkness of uncertainty, I seek solace in the radiant truth that the divine presence within me surpasses all worldly challenges.

Lord, I thank You for promising a bright future filled with hope and peace. I trust in Your love and guidance, knowing that You hold my destiny in Your hands. Help me to banish all fears about tomorrow and rely solely on Your truth and power. Today, I choose to rejoice in Your creation and embrace Your provision. Thank You for being my protector and provider, showering me with grace and glory. I am determined to run my race faithfully, empowered by Your love and strength. Through Jesus, I am more than a conqueror over every challenge.

Lead me to an abundant life, where Your presence brings joy and fulfillment. Your Holy Spirit within me secures my future. I fix my gaze on You, dismissing the voices of doom, for You alone determines my destiny. With faith, I press forward, leaving behind the past and embracing the glorious future You have prepared for me. In the divine rhythm of creation, it is written: *"Speak, and it shall be established."* (Job 22:28) As I embrace the sacred disciplines of fasting and prayer, I step into the realm of declaration and decree, where the words I utter are imbued with the power to manifest reality.

Day 26 — Miracle Mornings

I declare that the gates ordained by God swing wide before me, ushering forth blessing after blessing!

- Opportunities, handpicked by God, await my arrival.

- Marriage and friendships, sanctified by His grace, blossom in abundance.

- Businesses and/or employment opportunities ordained by Father God, flourish under the guiding light of my Lord and Saviour, Jesus.

- Streams of abundance burst forth into fruition, nourished by His hand.

- My nation and city/town, chosen by the Almighty, open their gates to receive the wisdom and grace that I bear as a witness.

- Even in my missteps, the hand of God weaves redemption into my life.

- With unwavering courage, I embark upon new adventures, knowing that I am divinely guided.

- The Lord shall bring to fruition that which He has ordained. As it is written: *"At the right time, I, the Lord, will make it happen"* (Is. 60:22).

When to Keep Quiet:

1. In the heat of anger - Prov. 14:17
2. When you don't have all the facts - Prov. 18:13
3. When you haven't verified the story - Deut. 17:6
4. If your words will offend a weaker person - 1 Cor. 8:11
5. If your words will be a poor reflection of the Lord or your friends and family - Peter 2:22-23
6. When you joke or make light of sin - Prov. 14:9
7. When you would be ashamed of your words later - Prov. 8:8

Day 26 — Miracle Mornings

8. When attempting to make light of Holy things - Ecc. 5:2
9. If your words would convey a wrong impression - Prov. 17:27
10. If the issue is none of your business - Prov. 14:10
11. If your words will damage someone's reputation - Prov. 16:27
12. When you don't feel any peace in your heart - Phil. 4:7
13. If your words will destroy a friendship - Prov. 25:28
14. When you are feeling critical - James 3:9
15. If you can't speak without yelling - Prov. 25:28
16. When it's time to listen - Prov. 13:1
17. If you may have to eat your words later - Prov. 18:21
18. If you have already said it more than once (then it becomes nagging) - Prov. 19:13
19. When you are tempted to flatter a wicked person - Prov. 24:24
20. When you're supposed to be working instead - Prov. 14:23

- Watch your words and hold your tongue; you'll save yourself a lot of grief.

- When words escalate to shouting, let silence be our peace (Prov. 25:28).

- When the time for listening arrives, let silence be our wisdom (Prov. 13:1).

- Lest our words sow seeds of regret, let silence be our caution (Prov. 18:21).

- When repetition breeds irritation, let silence be our patience (Prov. 19:13).

- To flatter not the wicked, let silence be our discernment (Prov. 24:24).

- In labour's hour, let silence be our diligence (Prov. 14:23).

- Let go of the furnace of anger, let silence be our shield (Prov. 14:17).

Day 27 — Miracle Mornings

Mighty Lord, I embrace Your divine promise as You speak through Your Word, declaring, *"Call to me, and I will answer you, and show you great and mighty things"* (Jer. 33:3). In fervent belief, I proclaim that *"everyone who calls on the Name of the Lord shall be saved"* (Rom. 10:13). Therefore, I lift my voice unto the heavens, invoking the sacred Name of Jesus for salvation, for the balm of healing, and for the liberation from all chains. I beseech You, O God, to unleash the prayers of Your faithful upon the earth. Let Your power resonate like thunder, let Your lightning blaze forth, and let Your righteous fire consume all that opposes Your divine will. May Your righteous judgement be swift and resolute, in the matchless Name of Jesus.

May the dominion of darkness crumble before Your might. Let the strongholds of Babylon fall, let the accuser's voice be silenced, and let the adversary be bound, in the majestic Name of Jesus.

I decree liberation for those ensnared by the shackles of this world's systems. Let the oppressed be set free from the powers that ensnare them, in the glorious Name of Jesus.

Expose the deeds of wicked leaders, and if their hearts remain hardened, remove them from their lofty thrones. Raise up righteous leaders, empowered by Your Spirit, to take their rightful place.

Thy Kingdom come; thy will be done on earth as it is in heaven!

Elevate my prayers to a higher realm. Propel my prayer life into a realm of divine encounter and spiritual breakthrough.

As the radiant Bride of Christ, adorned for the divine union with the Lamb, I embrace the hastening of time as the herald of His imminent return. The birth pangs of a new era quicken, signalling the Bridegroom's approach. In this appointed hour, I stand as a beacon of light, called forth *"for such a time as this,"* (Es. 4:14) to redeem the days shrouded in darkness.

Day   MIRACLE MORNINGS   27

Gracious Lord, I offer profound gratitude for Your boundless grace, which encompasses every facet of my being. Thank You for the encompassing salvation You have bestowed upon me. In Your infinite mercy, You infuse me with Your love, strengthening and soothing my spirit, dispelling all fear. Your Word is my steadfast anchor, reminding me of Your eternal presence and unwavering support. With You by my side, who dares stand against me? (Rom. 8:31) Grant me the resolve to stand firm upon Your promises and to commune with You ceaselessly.

Cultivate within me an unwavering faith, firmly rooted in Your truth. Engrave Your Word upon the tablets of my heart, that I may never stray from Your path. May Your truth be ever-present in my mind, shaping my thoughts and actions. Thank You for the living waters that flow abundantly from Your Spirit within me, quenching the parched lands of my soul. Guard me against the snares of fear and anxiety and embolden me to step forth into every calling You place before me, for You are my ever-present help in times of need (Ps. 46:1). Shield me from unseen dangers and grant me the discernment to perceive them from Your perspective. Guide me in walking according to Your Kingdom principles, led by the gentle promptings of Your Spirit. Increase my faith (Luke 17:5) daily as I immerse myself in Your Word and walk intimately with You. I am deeply cherished by You, and for that, I am eternally grateful. In the matchless Name of Jesus, I pray. Amen.

I align my heart with Your divine purpose, knowing that my journey shall culminate in peace, for I walk steadfastly in Your promises and power (Ps. 37:37). As the sands of time continue to slip through the hourglass, I embrace each moment as a sacred gift, poised to fulfill my destiny with unwavering faith and unyielding determination. Amen.

In humility, I will correct those who oppose me; perhaps God will grant them repentance so that they may know the truth (2 Tim. 2:25).

The fear of the Lord (i.e. to hate sin) is the instruction of wisdom, and before honour is humility (Prov. 15:33).

Day 28 — Miracle Mornings

When circumstances don't align as we hoped…

Rejection, failure, or setbacks may initially seem like detours from our objectives, but they often provide fertile ground for reflection, replenishment, and redirection. Amidst what feels like the demise of our aspirations, our true potential often begins to sprout.

If a door remains closed, it's simply not meant for us to enter. Sometimes, we find ourselves striving for goals that aren't truly aligned with God's desires for us and remember, He knows best. In our moments of distress, we unearth our greatest strength. Success isn't solely built on accomplishments but also on setbacks, frustrations, and fears yet to be conquered. Sometimes, a significant stumble is needed to gauge our position accurately. When it appears, we're being denied something worthwhile, it's merely a redirection towards something even better.

"After this I looked, and there before me was a door standing open in heaven. And the voice I had first heard speaking to me like a trumpet said, 'Come up here, and I will show you what must take place after this.'" (Rev. 4:1)

"Ask and it will be given to you; seek and you will find; knock and the door will be opened to you. For everyone who asks receives; the one who seeks finds; and to the one who knocks, the door will be opened." (Matt. 7:7-8)

"The earth is the Lord's, and everything in it, the world, and all who live in it; for he founded it on the seas and established it on the waters. Who may ascend the mountain of the Lord? Who may stand in his holy place? The one who has clean hands and a pure heart, who does not trust in an idol or swear by a false god. They will receive blessing from the Lord and vindication from God their Saviour. Such is the generation of those who seek him, who seek your face, God of Jacob. Lift up your heads, you gates; be lifted up, you ancient doors, that the King of glory may come in." (Ps. 24:1-7)

Day 28
MIRACLE MORNINGS

Heavenly Father,

Light up any shadows of past fears that linger within me, hindering the fullness of the life You've destined for me. Grant me the strength to release them and step boldly into the newness You offer each day. May Your unwavering love dispel every destructive fear, empowering me to fulfill Your divine purpose without hesitation or doubt. Guide my words and actions, that they may resonate with Your truth and love, touching the hearts of those I encounter. Grant me clarity, courage, and compassion as I navigate conversations, infusing them with Your presence and wisdom. Root out any lingering fears that threaten to obstruct Your liberty in my life. I surrender all control to You, desiring to be bound only by Your righteousness. Let Your perfect love reign in me, driving out all tormenting fears. Thank You, Lord, for Your promise to deliver me from every fear. In the mighty Name of Jesus, I pray. Amen.

Lord, grant me the discernment to heed Your gentle whispers, guiding me away from harm's way and towards paths of righteousness. Teach me to turn to prayer whenever fear or intuition signals danger, shielding me, my loved ones, and my friends from peril. Bestow upon us the wisdom to recognize and heed warnings, keeping us safe from the schemes of the enemy. Help me to surrender my understanding to Your omniscience, acknowledging Your sovereignty in every aspect of my life. Guard me against presumptuous sins, preventing them from gaining dominion over me. May I never presume to know everything without consulting You first, seeking Your truth above all else. Lead me daily by Your Holy Spirit, bearing fruit that reflects Your character - love, joy, peace, patience, kindness, goodness, faithfulness, gentleness, and self-control. Teach me the discipline of constant prayer, ensuring I remain aligned with Your will and timing in all things.

In Jesus' Name, I pray. Amen.

Day 29
Miracle Mornings

The presence of God accompanies me as I move through each day. Expectantly, I anticipate impactful divine appointments to bring healing, prophecy, salvation, deliverance, signs, wonders, and blessings wherever I go.

My prayers wield immense power, resonating with God's attentive ear and eliciting divine responses. God abundantly fulfills all my financial needs according to His gracious will.

I am liberated from the grip of sin, fully alive and committed to obeying God's commands.

Consistently, I am a conduit pipe for divine encounters, ushering others into transformative experiences with God.

Through Jesus, I am embraced with unconditional love and deemed worthy to receive God's blessings.

Each family member is showered with divine favour and enveloped in Jesus' profound love.

I respond to the devil's lies with resounding laughter, secure in the truth of God's promises.

With unwavering conviction, I decree that God is on my side, rendering defeat, discouragement, depression, and disappointment powerless over me.

Challenges are but avenues for adventure, and I exercise authority over them.

Speaking forth God's promises, I thwart all attacks, oppressions, and fears, ushering in His peace and fulfillment.

My Angels diligently execute God's will on my behalf, ensuring His promises manifest in my life.

Day 29

MIRACLE MORNINGS

S.W.B.D.D.

Sacrifice (an offering to Him)

Offer a daily sacrifice. Daily, there is something in us that we need to bring to Him. We are not legally bound by that, but the principle of connecting with Him is the same; we must connect with Him daily. Confess sins daily and be delivered.

Wisdom (ask and then receive it)

Wisdom-watching daily. Too often, we lean on our own understanding, but if we ask for wisdom, He will give us wisdom. The Word of God also says we must watch for it coming to our gate. So, it's not just asking for wisdom. Instead, watch so we can open the gate for wisdom.

Bread (ask for and thank Him for provision)

Ask for daily bread. Read Matthew 6. The Lord is going to bring the Body of Christ into a new way of praying to unlock the next level of provision that we need. Asking for our daily bread involves reviewing and presenting our needs daily.

Discern (both Him and evil)

Discern daily. Read Hebrews 5:12-14. We must discern the spiritual forces operating around us. We discern two ways: by the Word and by the Spirit of God. The daily sacrifice in which the Word becomes a cycle in your life unlocks spiritual discernment, and that's where reality comes in. You don't enter reality just by knowing the Word; you must discern by the Spirit. Spirit and truth together produce reality.

Die (of yourself for Him)

There's something in our lives that we have to die to daily. Read 1 Cor. 15:30-34. We can't come into resurrection without death, and that's why Paul said, *"Daily, I have to die."* (1 Cor. 15:31) We must be aware of what it is that we're trying to keep alive, daily, that God is trying to kill.

Day — MIRACLE MORNINGS — 30

Behold, I shall become a vessel of divine grace, a beacon of light in the darkness of souls. For it is written, *"He who wins souls is wise"* (Dan. 12:3), and thus, with fervent zeal, I embrace this sacred calling. The fire of God's love ignites within me, compelling me to walk the path of the Great Commission to embody the essence of Christ in this earthly realm. May my hands be instruments of healing, and my feet, messengers of service, as I traverse the journey set before me.

Let the veil be lifted from my eyes, O Lord, that I may perceive with clarity the mysteries of Your Kingdom. As it is written, *"The Lord will anoint my eyes with eye salve"* (Rev. 3:18), granting me vision akin to the majestic eagle, soaring above earthly confines. In your divine light, I shall discern the hidden snares laid by the adversary, for your strength, a conqueror in Your Name, fortifies me.

By the power vested in me through Christ, I break every chain of darkness that seeks to entangle my spirit. From the depths of my being, I cast off the shackles of witchcraft, hexes, and every form of demonic influence. I stand firm in the knowledge that I am liberated by the Blood of the Lamb, destined to inherit the blessings of generations past.

Behold, the gates of destiny swing wide before me, ordained by the hand of the Almighty. With the keys of the Kingdom in my grasp, I seal shut every portal of deceit and confusion, opening wide the floodgates of Heaven's favour. In this sacred covenant, I dwell beneath an open sky, guided by the divine hand towards my purpose.

Let the fellowship of the anointed encompass me, O Lord, as I walk the path of righteousness. Drawn to those who bear the mark of Your grace, I seek refuge within the community of true disciples. Rooted in the soil of divine truth, I flourish amidst the blest, shielded from the snares of the unrighteous.

Kindle within me, O Lord, the flame of first love, burning bright with devotion. Let my heart be a vessel of adoration, tender and responsive to Your divine presence. As a true worshipper, I offer unto You the sacrifice of a contrite heart, forever enamoured by Your boundless love.

Day 30 — Miracle Mornings

I recommit myself to praying for the things that need to be changed in this world. I will stand up against the enemy and say, "Enough is enough." The devil will not take over.

Grant unto me, O Lord, the gift of fervent prayer and unwavering intercession. As a watchman, I stand vigilant, calling Your divine will upon the earth. Anointed with the oil of intercession, I utter the sacred words that echo the prayers of the Son, ushering forth Your Kingdom come. May the nine fruits of the Spirit blossom within me as a testament to Your boundless grace. In humility and generosity, I extend my hand to those in need, embodying Christ's love in every deed. With patience and compassion, I tread the path of righteousness, a beacon of light amidst the shadows.

Grant me, O Lord, the spirit of wisdom and discernment, that I may lead Your flock (my family) with grace and humility. In reverence for Your Holy Name, I shun the darkness of sin, embracing the path of righteousness. Strengthened by Your divine guidance, I shepherd Your people (my family) towards the shores of salvation.

In the embrace of Your love, I find solace and refuge, for nothing can sever our bond. As it is written, *"For I am convinced that neither death nor life, neither angels nor demons, neither the present nor the future, nor any powers will be able to separate us from the love of God that is in Christ Jesus our Lord"* (Rom. 8:38-39). Forever cherished in Your sight, I am Your beloved child, eternally embraced by Your love.

I believe that when I pray in faith, strongholds are broken, territories and regions are transformed, and mountains move (Mark 11:24).

I declare that the enemy will be thrown down in the Name of Jesus. I bind (Matt. 18:18) all the enemy's works to deceive, steal, kill, destroy; I bind witchcraft, death, destruction, murder, poverty, injustice, division and any other thing that tries to stop the flow of God's glory in the earth, especially in my life and the lives of my family.

Day 31: Miracle Mornings

You are a strategic God, and You are no respecter of persons (Acts 10:34). I pray You will give me strategies to help me in every situation I face as I pursue the vision You have given me, just as You gave the patriarchs of the Old Testament:

- Like Isaac, grant me, Oh Lord, the strategy to prosper amidst economic turmoil (Gen. 26:12-14).

- As Jacob transitioned from humble beginnings to entrepreneurial success, light my path, Lord, to prosperity (Gen. 30).

- Endow me, Oh Lord, with Joseph's wisdom in economic stewardship, that I may transform nations (Gen. 41).

- Like Gideon, grant me, Oh Lord, the insight to triumph against overwhelming odds (Judges 7).

- Empower me, Oh Lord, with the divine wisdom to topple the walls of impossibility, as Joshua did at Jericho (Jos. 6).

- Bestow upon me, Oh Lord, the spirit of Moses, to lead others out of pain and bondage (Ex. 3-12).

- Like Elisha, equip me, Oh Lord, with strategies for community healing and financial freedom (2 Kings 2:19-22; 4:1-7).

- Light my path and show me, Oh Lord, the way, as You did for Nehemiah in the reconstruction of Jerusalem (Neh. 1-6).

- Fill me, Oh Lord, with the spirit of Elijah, to dismantle strongholds of darkness and oppression (1 Kings 18:17-46).

- As Daniel rose to prominence in Babylon, grant me, Oh Lord, the strategies to prosper in unfamiliar territories (Daniel chapters 1-2).

Day 31: Miracle Mornings

Recently, I was bemoaning past mistakes I had made in my lifetime. I had asked for forgiveness before, but felt remorseful again. The Lord said:

- "In a man's journey with Me, his faith is nourished when his questions about his circumstances are not answered. If they were answered, fear may obstruct his destiny."

- "Progress is hindered until you cease indulging in guilt over past actions. This impresses only you, as you mistake it for repentance."

- "'Woe is me' lacks the sincerity of 'Forgive me and guide me forward.' Dwelling in self-pity is an attempt at self-justification."

- "Genuine efforts to please Me involve not flaunting past mistakes as a symbol of defeat. Instead, learn from them to avoid repetition, bringing contentment to Me."

- "Expressing gratitude for actions contrary to My nature is akin to echoing an orphan's cry. Instead, acknowledge and appreciate My inherent attributes."

Thankfulness (in the first person of the Father)

"Thankfulness takes the sting out of adversity. That is why I have instructed you to give Me thanks for everything. There is an element of mystery in this transaction: You give Me thanks (regardless of your feelings), and I give you joy (regardless of your circumstances). This is a spiritual act of obedience - at times, blind obedience. To people who don't know Me intimately, it can seem irrational and even impossible to thank Me for heartrending hardships. Nonetheless, those who obey Me in this way are invariably blest, even though difficulties may remain. Thankfulness opens your heart to My presence and your mind to My thoughts. You may still be in the same place, with the same set of circumstances, but it is as if a light has been switched on, enabling you to see from My perspective. It is the Light of My Presence that removes the sting from adversity." (Eph. 5:20; Ps. 118:1; Ps. 89:15)

Miracle Mornings
Epilogue

Decreeing and declaring, above most other things, should create an understanding that we are broken and in need of a Saviour. To the world, brokenness is a currency of darkness but to be broken unto the Lord is one of the greatest advances we could aspire to do in faith. What does it mean to be truly broken unto the Lord? To be truly broken is to shed the veils of resentment and rebellion. It's to relinquish the ego's grip on our hearts and minds. We remain unbroken when we harbour resentment, take offence, or retaliate against the world's injustices. In the surrender of self-justification and defence, we find the first whispers of true brokenness.

Each trial, each moment of heartache and sorrow, is a chisel in the hands of God, sculpting our souls into vessels of humility and surrender. Watchman Nee spoke truth when he revealed that God's purpose is to reduce us, stripping away the illusions of self-sufficiency until all that remains is an open vessel, ready to be filled with the grace of the divine.

Upon the altar of transformation, let us offer ourselves, crying out, "Lord, break me, mould me, make me. You are the potter I am the clay." With each surrender, we make room for the indwelling of Holy Spirit, inviting divine guidance into our lives.

Are we prepared to embrace the journey of brokenness, to surrender our will to the greater wisdom of the divine? Let us not cling to the illusions of self but instead open our hearts to the transformative power of grace. In this surrender, we find the truest freedom, the deepest connection to Holy Spirit, and the power to serve in alignment with God's purpose for our lives.

So, I ask you now: "Are you willing to surrender? Are you ready to offer yourself upon the altar of transformation?" The choice is yours. A new vision awaits, a new freedom beckons and a new power stirs within. Will you answer the call?

Obviously, it goes without saying that my intent in writing a 31-day devotional is to provide you, the reader, with 31 days of material. Guess what? I have more material than there are days in the month! That said, here is some "extra stuff" for you. Enjoy!

Miracle Mornings

The Top 3 Spiritual Attacks:
• Living in fear instead of faith (1 John 4:18; fear invites tormentors).
• Lack of love (violates Jesus' greatest commandment).
• Speaking against and judging others (removes our authority to pray).

Solution To The 3 Attacks:
• Cast out the spirit of fear and its tormentors.
• Be filled with God's perfect love (for ourselves, God and others).
• Remove judgements against ourselves, God and others.

Self-Deliverance

Pray: If you are concerned about whether you need deliverance, close your eyes and pray. If you feel peace and no particular area comes to mind, that's good. We are to let the peace of God rule in our life. If a particular person or situation does stand out, consider this:

First: If you have opened a door to torment by sinning, picture the sin.
Feel: Feel the negative emotion in your gut.
Forgive: Forgive and/or receive forgiveness until it changes to peace. (If another person is involved, forgive them, too.) Now, yield and receive repentance as a gift. Yield to the Deliverer. If you still feel external pressure or oppression after you have peace in your heart, yield to Jesus (the deliverer in you), and welcome Him to rise up within you and push off any religious hitchhiker. Continue to yield to Him until you feel the pressure in the atmosphere lift. Once the oppression lifts, stay in the peace of God. The enemy can't touch the Fruit of the Spirit. If you accidentally lose your peace, receive forgiveness and you will feel peace again.

The Still Small Voice.

Be Still: Stop, Be Silent, and you will Hear.

"Then He said, 'Go out, and stand on the mountain before the Lord.' And behold, the Lord passed by, and a great and strong wind tore into the mountains and broke the rocks in pieces before the Lord, but the Lord was not in the wind; and after the wind an earthquake, but the Lord was not in the earthquake; and after the earthquake a fire, but the Lord was not in the fire; and after the fire a still small voice." (1 Kings 19:11-12)

Miracle Mornings

"Listen for God's voice in everything you do, everywhere you go; He's the one who will keep you on track." (Prov. 3:6)

"Whether you turn to the right or to the left, your ears will hear a voice behind you, saying, "This is the way; walk in it." (Is. 30:21)

"So Eli told Samuel, "Go and lie down, and if he calls you, say, 'Speak, Lord, for your servant is listening.'" (1 Sam. 3:9)

Five Tests You Need to Pass

1. **The Test of Time** - Patience; the Word.
2. **The Test of Faith** - God's presence is not contingent on the presence or absence of problems.
3. **The Test of Purity** - Purity is the way through prison to the palace.
4. **The Test of Forgiveness** - My future is bigger than my hurt.
5. **The Test of Diligence** - Do your best at each season before moving into the next one.

The anointing will always work better through you than for you. If you are not allowing God's anointing to flow through you because it hasn't done anything for you, you failed the last test.

Tests

1. Preceding any significant assignment lies a series of tests and challenges.
In my journey, I've discerned a pattern: just before embarking on a significant endeavour, whether in personal growth, ministry, or life events, I often encounter intense resistance. Initially perplexing, I've come to recognize this as a precursor to noteworthy divine interventions. Over time, I've learned to interpret such opposition as confirming divine involvement. Thus, amid spiritual warfare, I am assured that something substantial will unfold. This understanding fortifies my resolve, enabling me to persevere through formidable obstacles.

2. Tests follow the culmination of achievements.
Experience has taught me that moments of triumph are sometimes swiftly followed by assaults from adversarial forces. The enemy, relentless in his efforts, seeks to impede our progress, capitalizing on our vulnerability after our success. This phenomenon echoes narratives like

Elijah's ordeal after showcasing God's supremacy or Jesus' confrontation with demonic oppression following a profound encounter with divine glory. I've learned the importance of remaining vigilant after personal victories, guarding against unforeseen attacks that could derail my momentum.

3. Tests emerge between the pronouncement of a prophetic word and its realization.
Waiting for the fulfillment of a prophetic utterance constitutes one of the most arduous tests of faith. Often, the timing of these prophecies eludes our comprehension, leading to misconceptions about their imminent fruition. My own journey bears witness to the protracted intervals between revelation and realization, challenging my faith to its core. Reflecting on Abraham's decades-long wait for Isaac's birth and the subsequent trial of obedience underscores the necessity of patient endurance amid deferred promises. It underscores the imperative to discern both the timing and the interpretation of divine directives, trusting in their eventual fulfillment while remaining steadfast in faith.

4. Temptation exploits moments of vulnerability.
The Gospel narratives depict how temptation often strikes in moments of weakness or fatigue. Just as the devil confronted Jesus after His forty-day fast, believers find themselves assailed during moments of emotional frailty or physical exhaustion. Understanding the adversary's relentless nature dispels any notion of leniency during our struggles. Thus, cultivating supportive relationships within the Christian community is paramount, offering spiritual reinforcement in our weakest moments. Additionally, exercising caution in decision-making and communication while under emotional duress safeguards against succumbing to temptation.

5. Boredom begets susceptibility to temptation.
The account of King David's transgression in 2 Samuel 11 underscores how idleness can lead to moral lapses. Aimlessness often breeds discontent, leading individuals to seek gratification through illicit means. Maintaining a steadfast devotion to God is a bulwark against such temptations, infusing mundane moments with spiritual significance. By prioritizing intimacy with the divine over mere activity, one can navigate periods of monotony with purpose and resilience, thereby fortifying oneself for future challenges.

Miracle Mornings

6. Temptation arises when focus wavers from primary objectives.

Distractions pose a significant threat when they divert attention from core responsibilities and divine callings. Beyond spiritual devotion and familial obligations, each harbours a primary assignment deserving unwavering focus. Though not inherently sinful, succumbing to the allure of seemingly benign opportunities can detract from our overarching purpose. Recognizing this subtle deception, we must remain vigilant in safeguarding our focus, ensuring that essential priorities remain paramount. In doing so, we preserve our capacity to pursue God's best amidst competing demands. Ultimately, amid the trials and temptations of life's journey, I find solace in the assurance of divine presence and provision. Scripture reminds us of God's faithfulness in providing avenues of escape during testing times, offering comfort and sustenance through every trial.

Relationships:
- The Lord surrounds me with divine, peer-level relationships and companions who are honest, genuine, trustworthy, Godly, mutually beneficial and long-lasting.
- My friendships are God-given and are with people who will stick closer than a sibling.
- My peer-level relationships will be with those who love God and pray for and with each other when facing difficulties.

Family:
- The Father is enlarging my borders and territory while increasing me and my extended family with breakthrough blessings.
- I will provide for those I love and those in my household so that the Lord will see my faith and bless me.
- God is placing divine connections in my sphere of activity. He is giving me people I consider family who will pray for, support and love me.

Overcoming:
- I have Holy Spirit's power to overcome any hindering situation, ongoing problem, unexpected circumstances and challenges that I face.
- Every victim mentality is broken off me, and I am an overcomer by the Word of my testimony and by the Blood of the Lamb.
- I will recover all that the enemy has stolen, and I will walk in total freedom in Holy Spirit.

Miracle Mornings

Church:
- My church family and community is vibrant, powerful and anointed by God with the glory that brings breakthrough, healing, wholeness, deliverance, restoration and the supernatural.
- As I am planted in the household of faith and am submitted to other faithful believers, I will flourish, prosper and receive what the Father has destined for me.
- The Father is giving me pastors and leaders who are after His heart and who will skillfully lead, guide, and feed me as God has instructed them.

Revelation of God:
- I am receiving fresh revelation of the Father's heart, and I will align myself with His Word. I am receiving my portion.
- I am more than a conqueror through Christ, who loves me, and I am receiving daily breakthroughs.
- God is making the impossible possible because all things are possible with the Father.

Final Thoughts & Scriptures:

God will empower you to accomplish the impossible when you surrender to Him. He seeks those who will stand in the gap, be faithful witnesses, and say, 'Here am I! Send me.' Will you be that vessel for Him? (2 Chron. 16:9; Is. 6:8; Rev. 1:4-6)

His grace is more than sufficient for your needs. Seek it with a humble heart, and God will abundantly provide. (James 4:6; James 4:8-10; 2 Cor. 12:9)

Life's trials are inevitable, but don't let problem-solving consume you. Make your relationship with God a priority; seek His perspective and let your burdens fade in the light of eternity. (Ps. 32:8; Luke 10:41-42; Phil. 3:20-21)

God favours the humble - those who seek forgiveness, intercede faithfully and stand in the gap. Thank Him continually; it opens the door to unceasing prayer and communication with Him. (1 Thess. 5:16-18; James 4:8; Rom. 15:13)

Miracle Mornings

Rejoice in each day He has made, for within it lies precious gifts and opportunities for growth. Walk in thanksgiving, knowing He is with you always. (Ps. 118:24; Ps. 116:17; Ps. 118:28)

Author's Note:

As we complete this journey through *"Miracle Mornings"* I want to leave you with some guidelines for writing your own decrees. Though these words have been crafted with intention and care, it is vital to recognize that only you, in communion with Holy Spirit, know of the intricacies of your own life and the path ahead. Therefore, I offer you a framework to craft your own prayers, decrees, and declarations. These blank pages ahead are for you to lay bare your deepest desires and aspirations before God.

Yet, let us proceed with caution; our decrees must always align with the Word. Yes, you may decree healing and indeed, prosperity. However, let us not be so foolish as to dictate the specific outcomes we expect. God is not a mere servant of our worldly whims. He is the sovereign orchestrator of the universe, and:

"For My thoughts are not your thoughts, Nor are your ways My ways," says the Lord. For as the heavens are higher than the earth, So are My ways higher than your ways, And My thoughts than your thoughts." (Is. 55:8-9)

Let us instead approach our prayers with humility, trusting in His infinite wisdom and boundless love.

Go ahead then, with courage and conviction, for the power of creation rests within your words, based upon His. His Words are not ours to command, but to align with the sacred will of our Lord and Father.

Miracle Mornings
My Decree Prayers:

_____

_____

_____

_____

_____

_____

_____

_____

_____

_____

_____

_____

_____

_____

_____

_____

_____

_____

Miracle Mornings

Miracle Mornings

Miracle Mornings

Miracle Mornings
Decree the Word for Your Healing.

"Praise be to the Almighty! Let us bless the Lord with all that is within us, never forgetting His benevolent grace and mercy."

These words of exaltation from Psalm 103 resonate deeply within my soul, especially during trying times. I affirm that God, who heals all diseases, has indeed healed and renewed me. Just as He has done for me, He is ever ready to pour out His abundant goodness upon you, my friend, *"for such a time as this."* (Es. 4:4) Rest assured, He reigns sovereignty upon His throne, and your destiny remains secure.

In the face of any storm, I encourage you to lift your gaze to the heavens and boldly proclaim the Scriptures - let their truth resound! Nothing is impossible with God, and we are more than conquerors through Christ's love. Let us diligently capture every thought that dares to challenge the supremacy of God's Word and steadfastly fix our hearts on envisioning His boundless best for us. As you immerse yourself in these healing declarations, may God infuse His divine power into your natural being, leading you to new heights of faith, healing, and restoration.

- For the Lord is the one who heals me. (Ex. 15:26)
- My days shall be 120 years, and I will enjoy good health. (Gen. 6:3; 3 John 2)
- I shall come to my grave in a full age, like as a shock of corn comes in his season. (Gen. 15:15)
- I shall come to the grave at a full age, like a sheaf of grain ripens in its season. (Job 5:26)
- When God sees the Blood, He will pass over me; and the plague shall not be on me to destroy me. (Ex. 12:13)
- I shall serve the Lord my God, and He will bless my bread and my water. And He will take sickness away from the midst of me. (Ex. 23:25-26)
- And the Lord will take away from me all sickness and will not afflict me with the terrible diseases of Egypt. (Deut. 7:15)
- And I shall live long on the earth, and it shall be well with me. (Deut. 11:9, 21)
- You have turned the curse into a blessing because You love me. (Deut. 23:5; Neh. 13:2)

Miracle Mornings

- Christ has redeemed me from the curse of the Law, and no evil or sickness shall befall me. (Gal. 3:13; Ps. 91:10)
- As my days, so shall my strength be. (Deut. 33:25)
- You have found a ransom for me, and my flesh shall be fresher than a child's. (Job 33:24-25)
- You have healed me and brought up my soul from the grave; You have kept me alive. (Ps. 30:1-3)
- You give me strength and blest me with peace. (Ps. 29:11)
- You will preserve me and keep me alive. (Ps. 41:2)
- You strengthen me upon the bed of languishing; You restore me in my sickbed. (Ps. 41:3)
- You are the health of my countenance and my God. (Ps. 43:5)
- No plague shall come near my dwelling. (Ps. 91:10)
- You will satisfy me with long life. (Ps. 91:16)
- You heal all my diseases. (Ps. 103:3)
- You sent Your Word and healed me and delivered me from my destructions. (Ps. 107:20)
- I shall not die, but live, and declare Your works. (Ps. 118:17)
- You heal my broken heart and bind up my wounds. (Ps. 147:3)
- The years of my life shall be many. (Prov. 4:10)
- Trusting You brings health to my navel and marrow to my bones. (Prov. 3:8)
- Your Words are life to me, health, and medicine to all my flesh. (Prov. 4:22)
- Your good report makes my bones fat. (Prov. 15:30)
- Your pleasant Words are sweet to my soul and health to my bones. (Prov. 16:24)
- Your joy is my strength. (Neh. 8:10; Prov. 17:22)
- The eyes of the blind shall be opened, and the ears of the deaf unstopped. The tongue of the dumb shall sing. (Is. 35:5; 32:3)
- The lame shall leap like a deer, and the tongue of the stammerers shall speak plainly. (Is. 35:6; 32:4)
- You recover me and make me live. You are ready to save me. (Is. 38:16, 20)
- You give power to the faint and renew strength. You strengthen and help me. (Is. 40:29; 40:31; 41:10)
- You bore my griefs and carried my sorrows. By Your stripes, I am healed. (Is. 53:4-5)
- You healed me. (Is. 57:19)

Miracle Mornings

My light breaks forth as the morning, and my health springs forth speedily. (Is. 58:8)
- You heal me and bind up my wounds. (Jer. 30:17)
- You bring health and cure, and reveal unto me the abundance of peace and truth. (Jer. 33:6)
- You bind up that which was broken and strengthen that which was sick. (Ezek. 34:16)
- You cause breath to enter into me, and I shall live. You put Your Spirit in me, and I shall live. (Ezek. 37:5, 14)
- I seek You, and I shall live. (Amos 5:4)
- You have arisen with healing in Your wings. (Mal. 4:2)
- I will be clean. (Matt. 8:3)
- You took my infirmities... You bore my sicknesses. (Matt. 8:17)
- You are the Lord, my physician. (Matt. 9:12)
- You are moved with compassion toward the sick, and You heal me. (Matt. 14:14)
- You heal all manner of sickness and all manner of disease. (Matt. 4:23)
- According to my faith, be it unto me. (Matt. 9:29)
- You give me power and authority... to heal all manner of sickness and all manner of disease. (Matt. 10:1)
- You healed them all. (Matt. 12:15)
- As many as touch You are made perfectly whole. (Matt. 14:36)
- Healing is the children's bread. (Matt. 15:26)
- You do all things well... You make the deaf to hear and the dumb to speak. (Mark 7:37)
- All things are possible to me because I believe. (Mark 9:23; 11:23-24)
- When hands are laid on me, I recover. (Mark 16:18)
- Your anointing heals... delivers... recovers sight... and sets at liberty. (Luke 4:18; Is. 61:1)
- You heal all those who have need of healing. (Luke 9:11)
- You did not come to destroy men's lives, but to save them. (Lk. 9:56)
- You give me authority... over all the power of the enemy. 0(Luke 10:19)
- Sickness is satanic bondage, and I am loosed today. (Luke 13:16)
- In You is life. (John 1:4)
- You are the bread of life... You give me life. (John 6:33, 35)
- The Words that You speak unto me are spirit and life. (John 6:63)
- You came that I may have life and that I may have it more abundantly. (John 10:10)

Miracle Mornings

- You are the resurrection and the life. (John 11:25)
- If I ask anything in Your Name, You will do it." (John 14:14)
- Faith in Your Name makes me strong and gives me perfect soundness. (Acts 3:16)
- You stretch forth Your hand to heal. (Acts 4:30)
- You make me whole. (Acts 9:34)
- You do good and heal all that are oppressed by the devil. (Acts 10:38)
- Your power causes diseases to depart from me. (Acts 19:12)
- The law of the Spirit of life in You has made me free. (Rom. 8:2)
- The same Spirit that raised You from the dead now lives in me. (Rom. 8:11).
- My body is a member of You... the temple of Your Spirit. (1 Cor. 6:15, 19-20).
- I rightly discern Your body... and judge myself to be saved, healed, and delivered by You. (1 Cor. 11:29-31)
- You have set gifts of healing in Your Body. (1 Cor. 12:28)
- Your life is made manifest in my mortal flesh. (2 Cor. 4:10-11)
- You have delivered me... and continue to deliver me. (2 Cor. 1:10)
- You have given me Your Name and put all things under Your feet. (Eph. 1:21-22)
- You want it to be well with me... and live long on the earth. (Eph. 6:3)
- You have delivered me from the power of darkness. (Col. 1:13)
- You will deliver me from every evil work. (2 Tim. 4:18)
- You tasted death for me... destroyed the devil... and delivered me from fear and bondage. (Heb. 2:9, 14-15)

- You wash my body with pure water. (Heb. 10:22; Eph. 5:26)
- Lift up the weak hands... let it be healed. (Heb. 12:12-13)
- Let the elders anoint me and pray for me... and You will raise me up. (James 5:14-15)
- As I pray for others, You heal me. (James 5:16)
- By Your stripes I was healed. (1 Peter 2:24)
- Your divine power has given unto me all things that pertain unto life and godliness. (2 Peter 1:3)
- Whosoever will, let him come and take of the water of life freely. (Rev. 22:17)
- You wish above all things that I may prosper and be in health. (3 John 2)

MIRACLE
MORNINGS
Word Confessions
- I have purposed that my mouth shall not transgress. (Ps. 17:3)
- Let the words of my mouth, and the meditation of my heart, be acceptable in thy sight, O Lord, my strength and my redeemer. (Ps. 19:14)
- Set a guard, O Lord, before my mouth; keep watch at the door of my lips. (Ps. 141:3)
- Hear, for I will speak excellent and princely things; and the opening of my lips shall be for right things. For my mouth shall utter truth, and wrongdoing is detestable and loathsome to my lips. All the words of my mouth are righteous; there is nothing contrary to truth or crooked in them. (Prov. 8:6-8)
- A gentle answer turns away wrath, but harsh words stir up anger. (Prov. 15:1)
- Death and life are in the power of the tongue; and they that love it shall eat the fruit thereof. (Prov. 18:21)
- For by thy words thou shalt be justified, and by thy words thou shalt be condemned. (Matt. 12:37)
- My mouth is a "life-giving well." (Prov. 10:11)
- A good man out of the good treasure of his heart bringeth forth that which is good; and an evil man out of the evil treasure of his heart bringeth forth that which is evil; for out of the abundance of the heart his mouth speaketh. (Luke 6:45)
- I shall eat good by the fruit of my mouth. I guard my mouth and keep my life. (Prov. 13:2-3)
- I have a wholesome tongue, and it is a tree of life. (Prov. 15:4)
- I guard my mouth and my tongue keeps me from trouble. (Prov. 21:23)
- My words are not stout against the Lord. (Mal. 3:13)
- I never bind anyone with the words of my mouth. (Matt. 18:18)
- I am always a positive encourager. I edify and build up; I never tear down or destroy. (Rom. 15:2)
- I speak the truth of the Word of God in love and I grow up into the Lord Jesus Christ in all things. (Eph. 4:15)
- I do not offend anyone with my words, and therefore I have a fully developed character, able to control my whole body and to curb my entire nature. (James 3:2)
- I do all things without grumbling, faultfinding, complaining, questioning or doubting. (Phil. 2:14)

Miracle Mornings

- I let no corrupt communication proceed out of my mouth, but that which is good to edifying, that it may minister grace to the hearer. I grieve not the Holy Spirit of God, whereby I am sealed unto the day of redemption. I let all bitterness, and wrath, and anger, and clamour, and evil speaking, be put away from me: And I am kind to others, tender hearted, forgiving one another, even as God for Christ's sake has forgiven me. (Eph. 4:29-32)
- Wherefore, I am swift to hear, slow to speak, slow to wrath. For the wrath of man worketh not the righteousness of God. (James 1:19-20 KJV)

Miracle Mornings

I will end this book with a page from Jennifer LeClaire's, *"The Prophet's Devotional."*

"MARCH 27

Releasing Prophetic Decrees

"Thou shalt also decree a thing, and it shall be established unto thee: and the light shall shine upon thy ways" (Job 22:28 KJV).

Just as prophets are called to a priesthood, prophets are also called to a kingship. Remember, Peter tells us we are a royal priesthood (see 1 Peter 2:9). Priests make intercession. Kings make decrees.* We have to know when to shift from interceding on our knees to standing with decrees. Prophets are well equipped to follow the Holy Spirit's leadership to make that shift, but we need to understand the power of a decree.

Different translations shed interesting light on Job 22:28. For example, the New International Version tells us, *"What you decide on will be done, and light will shine on your ways."* The Contemporary English Version puts it this way: *"He will do whatever you ask, and life will be bright."*

The Amplified Bible, Classic Edition expounds on this truth a little more: *"You shall also decide and decree a thing, and it shall be established for you; and the light [of God's favour] shall shine upon your ways."* And The Message assures, *"You'll decide what you want and it will happen; your life will be bathed in light."*

Prophetic decrees are decrees that emanate from your anointed mouth through a Holy Spirit-inspired utterance. It could be a Scripture the Holy Spirit drops in your spirit. Or it could be prophetic wisdom that He fills your mouth with as you set out to pray. In a moment, you could be in a priestly role petitioning, and in the next moment you could be in a kingly role decreeing.

---

* Note: I wrote about the fact that we are both Priests and Kings in Volume one of my *"Life is a Test"* series, Sept. 22 & 23.

Miracle Mornings

When we decree the written Word of God or release prophetic decrees, we are standing on solid ground and results are guaranteed because, again, God's Word does not return to Him void. It accomplishes what He sends it to do through you (see Is. 55:10-11). Your carnal nature will decree what it wants, what the devil wants - anything but what God wants. Your spirit man will decree the will of the Lord.

Prayer

Father, in the name of Jesus, help me navigate the realm of intercession with an understanding of the power of a decree. Lead me to exchange the priest's mantle for the king's mantle when I need to shift an atmosphere with Spirit-inspired words that enforce Your rule of law."*

This quote from Jennifer's book gives complete credence to what you have just read in my book, and credence to this scripture which I have mentioned before:

"Death and life are in the power of the tongue, And those who love it will eat its fruit." (Prov. 18:21)

In conclusion, the life that we're living and the life that we are going to live in the future is largely determined by the Words that we speak, and they come from what's in our hearts. That being the case, what is in our hearts (it should be the Word!) and what will we speak?

"For out of the abundance of the heart the mouth speaks." (Matt. 12:34)

---

* **Doc's Book Cub: *"The Prophet's Devotional"*** by Jennifer LeClaire. Destiny Image Publishers. Shippensburg, PA USA. Copyright 2021. Page 104.

Miracle Mornings

Miracle Mornings

Who is "Doc"?

Dr. S. R. Watkins BBA Th.B DPM Ph.D is a distinguished entrepreneur and educator who has dedicated a profound 40-year career to enriching lives through spiritual and professional growth. His commitment to this mission is unwavering, evidenced by his Ph.D. in Ministerial Studies, earned through his seminal work *"Biblical Economics 101: Living Under God's Financial Blessings."* In addition to his Ph.D, Dr. Watkins has earned a Bachelor of Business Administration and a Doctorate in Practical Ministry (Leadership).

At the core of Dr. Watkins' mission is a deep-seated commitment to serving others. His teachings in biblical economics, excellence training, and Christian business principles are not just theoretical, but are designed to empower individuals and organizations in practical ways. As a Financial/Operational Pastor, Dr. Watkins leverages his strategic planning and business consulting skills to guide his clients toward sustainable success. His extensive expertise has been shared with a wide range of entities, including entrepreneurial ventures, marketplace ministries, churches, and charitable organizations. Dr. Watkins' business acumen is evident in his ownership and management of a half dozen businesses during his career. His influence extends internationally as he teaches and hosts conferences, particularly in Rwanda, in partnership with Compassion Canada. Among his literary contributions are the five-volume *"Life is a Test: Hope in a Confusing World"* series and *"Miracle Mornings: 31 Days of Declarations and Devotions."* He will be write and publish more books in the future.

A licensed minister of the Gospel with the International Association of Ministries in Calgary, Alberta, Dr. Watkins is also commissioned by the Global Spheres Centre in Corinth, Texas, as a Business Apostle, Deliverance Minister, and Christian Author. His leadership and commitment to spiritual and community development are reflected in his memberships with the Global Council of Nations, the Global Trans-formation Project, the Canadian and International Coalition of Apostolic Leaders, the International Society of Deliverance Min-isters, and the Calgary Christian Connect Group. Dr. Watkins' life work is a testament to his unwavering devotion to uplifting others through faith and leadership.

Miracle Mornings

Outside his professional life, Dr. Watkins is an active individual with diverse interests, hobbies, and volunteer work. He enjoys swimming, hiking, camping, skiing, fitness, fine dining, gardening, rodeos, chuckwagon racing, and collecting antiques and Western art. His love for learning is evident as he reads one to two books a week! He is a Life Member and past President (5 terms) of the Trail Riders of the Canadian Rockies. For information about his teaching classes and consulting, contact him at info@newstartministries.ca.
(Written by Fred Schuman, Renewal Counselling, Calgary, AB.)

What's up with "Doc"?

Several years ago, I worked at a Christian summer camp here in Alberta. Apparently, it is customary for everyone (including staff) to be given a nickname. Mine was "Doc" (because of my education) and they gave me no choice in the matter; the name stuck. I seldom use my first name anymore because people often do not spell it correctly and/or tend to shorten it, (which I do not like) so "Doc" is easy to remember, and pretty hard to misspell.

Doc's Book Club

An expression says that "every man has one vice." I have one books! Out of my vast library (would you believe I have ten bookcases? Six of which are eight feet tall), I have read over 2,000 nonfiction Christian books, researched/written over 130 essays, and authored seven books, with more to write! As much as I believe that the Word of God (the Bible) is the final declaration on issues and should not be "interpreted" (just read it!), reading from good authors can educate and confirm the Word.

First and foremost, the books that I recommend provide a biblical perspective on life's challenges, such as financial struggles, relationship issues, health crises, and spiritual doubts. Each book is carefully selected to teach biblical truths about perseverance and faith in these difficult times, helping readers find hope and strength in God. These books also help readers to understand that God is sovereign and that all things work together for good for those who love God and are called according to his purpose. This will help readers maintain a biblical worldview and understand that their struggles serve a purpose and that God is in control.

Miracle Mornings

The books I recommend are also designed to be practical and actionable. They offer specific steps and strategies we can use to navigate life's challenges. For instance, they might offer advice on managing stress, building healthy relationships, or finding peace in times of uncertainty. These books help readers understand that God has a purpose for their lives and is working for their good. They also provide practical guidance on developing a positive mindset and maintaining a healthy perspective on life's challenges. This will empower readers to take control of their lives and make positive changes.

Furthermore, the books that I suggest promote hope and encouragement. They help readers understand that even in the darkest times, there is always hope. They provide biblical teaching on the importance of hope and the power of positive thinking. They also help readers grasp that God is always with us and at work for our good. This will help readers maintain a positive attitude, even in difficult times, and trust the Lord no matter the circumstances.

These books are rich in content and written in an easy-to-understand language, making them accessible to readers of all levels of biblical knowledge. They are organized and have a logical structure, ensuring a smooth reading experience for everyone.

In conclusion, Doc's Book Club is not just a resource but a catalyst for transformation. For Christian readers seeking biblical insights and practical guidance for life's challenges, the books we recommend offer a unique opportunity. They provide a biblical perspective, are actionable, and promote hope and encouragement. Whether you read all thirty or even half of them, you will undoubtedly be blessed with a renewed perspective and strengthened faith.

Prayers Answered - Graham Cooke
Access Granted - Steve Holmstrom
Christians Going to Hell - Seung Woo Byun
The Psychology of Totalitarianism - Dr. Mattias Desmet
Multiply your God-given Potential - John Bevere
The Return of the Gods - Jonathan Cahn
Resilient: Restoring your Weary Soul in these Turbulent Times - John Eldredge

Miracle Mornings

The Final Reformation and Great Awakening - Dr. Bill Hamon
The Authority of the Believer - Kenneth Hagin
Battlefield of the Mind - Joyce Meyer
Becoming a Millionaire God's Way - Dr. C. Thomas Anderson
Blessing or Curse - Derek Prince
The Blessing - Kenneth Copeland
Change Agent - Os Hillman
Deceived; Who Me? - Craig Hill
Failing Forward - John C. Maxwell
Five Wealth Secrets 96% of Us Don't Know - Craig Hill
The Apostolic Church Arising - Dr. Robert Heidler and Dr. Chuck Pierce
Hello Tomorrow - Dr. Cindy Trimm
How to Reach Your Life Goals - Dr. Peter Daniels
Living Your Strengths - Donald O. Clifton
Managing God's Mutual Funds - Kenneth Copeland
The Millionaire Mind - Thomas J. Stanley & William D. Danko
The Prayer of Jabez - Bruce Wilkinson
Possessing Your Inheritance - Chuck D Pierce and Rebecca Wagner Sytsema
Set Yourself Free - Dr. Robert Heidler
Power in Praise - Merlin Carothers
Put Your Dream to the Test - John Maxwell
Principle of the Path - Andy Stanley
The Purpose Driven Life - Rick Warren
The Power of a Parent's Blessing - Craig Hill
Re-Ordering Your Day - Chuck D. Pierce, Ed.
The Messianic Church Arising - Dr. Robert Heidler
Pagan Christianity? - Frank Viola
The Secrets of the Secret Place - Bob Sorge
Receive Your Healing and Reclaim Your Health - Cal Pierce
Redeeming the Time - Chuck D. Pierce
The Tongue - A Creative Force - Charles Capps
Wealth, Riches and Money - Craig Hill & Earl Pitts
A More Excellent Way To Be In Health - Dr. Henry W. Wright
The Invisible War; what every believer needs to know about satan, demons, and spiritual warfare - Chip Ingram
The 15 Invaluable Laws of Growth - John Maxwell
Unshackled: Breaking the Strongholds of Your Past To Receive Complete Deliverance - Kathy DeGraw

Miracle Mornings

Operating in the Courts of Heaven - Robert Henderson
Humility - Andrew Murray
An Audience of One - R.T. Kendall
Releasing Heaven on Earth - Rev. Dr. Alistair Petrie
God's Footprint in Business - Rev. Dr. Alistair Petrie
The Book of Acts - Dr. Peter Wagner
Discover Your Spiritual Gifts - Dr. Peter Wagner
Praying with Power - Dr. Peter Wagner
This Changes Everything - Dr. Peter Wagner
Rome's Anathemas - Dr. Selwyn Stevens
Dealing with Curses and Iniquities - Dr. Selwyn Stevens
Signs and Symbols - Dr. Selwyn Stevens
Unmasking Freemasonry - Dr. Selwyn Stevens
Blessing or Curse - Derek Prince
Thou Shalt Cast out Demons - Derek Prince
Note: I am constantly updating this list. A current one can be found on my website.

"Doc"

"Wisdom is the principal thing; therefore, get wisdom. And in all your getting, get understanding" (Prov. 4:7).

Miracle Mornings
Favourite Authors:

My book club features a diverse range of authors, each bringing unique perspectives and insights. Some of the esteemed authors I recommend include:

Dr. Chuck Pierce, Dr. Robert Heidler, Dr. Jerry Savelle, Craig Hill, Jesse Duplantis, Dr. Peter Wagner, Dr. Selwyn Stevens, Barbara Wentrouble, Derek Prince, Rev. Dr. Alistair Petrie, Kenneth Hagan, John Avanzini, Cal Pierce, R. T. Kendall, John Maxwell, Dr. Joseph Mattera, Steve Holmstrom, Jonathan Cahn, Rick Warren, Dr. Peter Daniels, John Polis, Keith Moore, Dr. Che Ahn, John Bevere, Cindy Jacobs, Robert Henderson, Dr. Russ Moyer, Dennis Peacocke, Graham Cooke and Dr. Henry Wright. This diverse lineup ensures that our book club caters to a wide range of interests and needs within the Christian community.

Additional Books by S. R. Watkins

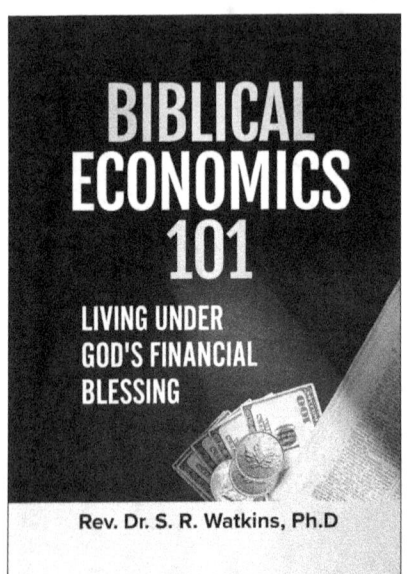

"This has to be the most balanced and useful summary of this topic I have come across. The clarity of his thinking and explanations of what Scripture teaches is to be highly commended and needs to be used widely to educate God's people about the issue of money, wealth and the Kingdom benefits that should accrue for this wise teaching.
I look forward to reports of the wide use of this book and reports of God's blessings on its use."

Selwyn Stevens, Ph.D (Bib St.); D. Min.
President, Jubilee Resources
International Inc., jubileeresources.org

"Religion and a poverty mindset are used in a powerful way to hinder Christians from receiving God's blessings for their lives! These people are often captured by the wrong use of scriptures. Believers are conditioned to believe that having finances will prevent them from being spiritual. Much of this teaching came from Greek philosophy and not from God's Word.

Dr. Stuart R. Watkins in his book, Biblical Economics 101: Living Under God's Financial Blessing, gives a Biblical understanding of God's plan for wealth. He destroys the cynicism of those who reject Kingdom prosperity. A fresh understanding of Kingdom wealth frees the reader to partner with God for transformation in the earth. Your life will be filled with the blessings of the Lord when you implement the principles found in Biblical Economics 101. Get ready to increase and multiply your finances for Kingdom purposes!"

Barbara Wentroble
President, International Breakthrough Ministries (IbM)
President, Breakthrough Business Leaders (BBL)
Author, *Becoming a Wealth Creator; Prophetic Intercession; Fighting for Your Prophetic Promises; Council Room of the Lord Series.*

"In these pages, Dr. Watkins presents us with a Scripturally sound, well-researched, and highly practical handbook on how to understand and steward the finances God entrusts to us. But this book is more than simply the handling of finances. This is an authentic explanation of money and resourcing based on a Biblical worldview that explains why there is spiritual warfare and much misunderstanding over all finances - especially when used for Kingdom purposes. God has no problem with money - we do! But to understand the history and Biblical grasp of finances and economics is essential if the use of finances and wealth is to be seen as a crucial element in fulfilling the final chapters of the Great Commission.

This book is a strategic resource for everyone in the Body of Christ. Along with pen and paper and a Bible in hand, be prepared to take notes while being challenged, informed, and prepared for a study in Biblical economics that is life-changing!"

Rev. Dr. Alistair P. Petrie
Pastor - Author
Executive Director
Partnership Ministries
www.partnershipministries.org

"Money is one of those taboo subjects most people do not want to discuss let alone explore more deeply. This subject is rarely taught on for a variety of reasons and Scriptures used are often misinterpreted. As a result, many are held back from walking in freedom in this area.

Dr. Watkins in his book, Biblical Economics 101: Living Under God's Financial Blessing, constructs a strong foundation to understand more accurately and succinctly what Scriptures have to say about money, wealth, and living with an understanding of a Kingdom economy. He provides insightful clarity to this subject, practical examples and addresses incorrect beliefs and mindsets passed along through incorrect teaching and application of the Word. Readers will find themselves on a new journey of discovery and increasing freedom as they apply the principles contained in this book and discover in new ways how they can partner with the Lord for Kingdom and eternal purposes."

Ray Borg
Ministry & Church Liaison, Financial Discipleship Canada
Compasscanada.org and notmine.ca
Co-author - *"It's Not About the Money - Unmasking Mammon"*

Discover the *"Life is a Test"* series. Five volumes packed full of Biblical Wisdom and Spiritual Insights about every day life.

In this Volume 1 edition, discover:
- Love; what is it?
- Spiritual Warfare
- Psalm 23, in depth
- The Three Baptisms
- Speaking in Tongues
- The Sound of the Shofar
- The Six Major Anointings of God
- Comparing Todays Churches to Acts
- The 8 Foundations of Being a Christian

"This is a great book! When you read it, you feel like you are sitting beside the author and he is talking to you. Read it! You will be glad you did!"
Chester Henry, Halifax NS

5 out of 5 stars!
"I so love my daily devotional which is a quick read but full of very deep meaning. I love how the book always compares to our day to day "stuff" but can always pull it back to the Bible. I like this comparison. The "Life is a Test" message is very thought-provoking. I truly, truly enjoyed this. I am looking forward to the next edition. Thanks so much for sharing this book with the world. I enjoy growing in God."

Linda Coyle, Arlington, TX.

4 out of 5 stars - life from many angles
"Dr. Stuart Watkins has presented us with a devotional that examines life from many angles. The devotional has a piercing style for how it challenges the reader to hear God's words from scripture and then immediately check our lives for how well we are listening.

But it is not a "supposed to" devotional! This book is not about digging up should after should. Watkins weaves the truths of scripture into the unfolding fabric of daily events, thoughts, emotions and choices. It reads as from a man who has experienced deep hardships in life yet remains convinced of God's goodness and is willing to wait on God patiently enough to receive his goodness again and again. His life lessons will speak to you. Stuart Watkins encourages you forward to victorious Christian living."

Dr. Don MacNaughton, Ph.D, Water Valley, AB.

www.newstartministries.ca

In this Volume 2 edition, discover:

- Angels
- The Ecclesia
- Satan/Demons
- God's Calendar
- Familiar Spirits
- Love and Hope
- Tips for Daily Success
- Faith is the way of Life.
- How to hear from God
- How to Minister to the Sick
- What on earth is God doing?
- The Nine Fruits of the Spirit
- You are a Hebrew - Like Jesus!
- The Seven Mountain Dominion

5 out of 5 stars!

"Highly recommend! Dr. Watkins presents clear, thought-provoking questions that will have you re-evaluating your preconceived notions of faith, community, and our Christianity as individuals. Through a biblical foundation in each daily devotion, Dr. Watkins provides biblical evidence, with a concise and clear summary to reflect on. Prepare to be challenged, as you embark on a year-long journey to understand more about who God is, and how He directs us to live day to day."

J. Henry, Toronto, ON.

"It's just one of those books that you don't want to put down and you are so glad that you bought! It only takes five minutes a day and with that you can be filled with enough wisdom and peace to get you through the week. The part I like the best is that it is Bible-based about everything that the author says. I can't wait for volume three to be published. I will definitely be buying a copy of it!"

S. L. Johnston, Fort Worth, TX.

"This book has opened my eyes, to many things about my walk with Jesus that I never knew. It was completely revelational, and it only takes five minutes a day to read and another five minutes to pray into it. It has just changed my life. Thank you so much, sir, for writing such a wonderful inspiring book!

John Cormack, Sheridan WY.

In this Volume 3 edition, discover:

- Leadership
- Life After Death
- The Wilderness
- Who can Ascend?
- Cleansing the Land
- The Gifts of the Spirit
- Hosting His Presence
- Who You Are in Christ
- The Secret Things of God
- Long life? Do these things...
- Who your Greatest Enemy Is
- The Restoration of the Church
- Revival and the Remnant Church

"Life is a Test: Hope in a Confusing World" by S. R. Watkins is a beautifully written devotional that provides much-needed encouragement in our daily walk of faith and speaks directly to the soul. Each page is filled with wisdom, insight, and biblical truth that speaks directly to the heart. In a world filled with uncertainty, this book serves as a guiding light, reminding us that God is always in control. The reflections are uplifting, thought-provoking, and easy to apply to everyday life. The book is structured in a way that makes it easy to read daily, providing spiritual nourishment in small but powerful doses. A must-read for anyone seeking spiritual growth and renewed hope"
Shelia Wilson, Vancouver, B.C.

"Dr. Watkins has done it again with *Life is a Test: Hope in a Confusing World,* Volume 3! This book is an excellent resource for those looking for daily inspiration rooted in faith. The short yet powerful insights challenge readers to trust God through trials and embrace His plan with confidence. Watkins' ability to weave scripture with practical wisdom makes this devotional both engaging and transformative. Whether you read it first thing in the morning or before bed, you'll walk away encouraged and uplifted. I loved it! A true gem!"
John Wickmore, Bury St. Edmunds, UK

"A Powerful and Uplifting Read! This book is a breath of fresh air for anyone feeling overwhelmed by the uncertainties of life. *Life is a Test: Hope in a Confusing World* offers a daily dose of wisdom that strengthens faith and brings perspective to difficult situations. S. R. Watkins masterfully reminds us that challenges are not obstacles but opportunities for spiritual growth. The reflections are deeply insightful, encouraging readers to persevere with faith, hope, and trust in God's timing. I highly recommend this book for personal devotion or as a gift to encourage a friend! Definitely 5 Stars!"
J. R. Armstrong, Baton Rouge, LA

In this Volume 4 edition, discover:
- Nehemiah's Anointing
- The Power of Blessing
- Going Through a Storm
- The Seven Spirits of God
- Why Christians Fail to Receive
- Worship; the Key to His Presence
- Jesus Commanded Us To Do This
- Five Common Myths About Salvation
- The Church Then and Today; What Went Wrong?
- Step-by-step with God: Achieving Your Life Vision
- 32 Ways of Walking in the Power of Jesus
- What Has the Western Church Missed?

"Life is a Test: Hope in a Confusing World (Volume Four) is a masterpiece of spiritual clarity. Rev. Dr. S. R. Watkins delivers timeless wisdom for modern believers, blending Scripture with real-life application. Each daily reading inspires faith, resilience, and renewed focus on God's purpose. It's a daily must-read for those seeking strength in uncertain times."
Jose Ferreira, Houston, TX

"Every page of this book reminds the reader that God is faithful in every season. Volume Four of Life is a Test offers encouragement, correction, and hope with biblical truth and heartfelt sincerity. I just bought this volume 4 edition, and now I want to get the other ones too!"

Joanne Mason
Vancouver, B.C.

In this Volume 5 edition, (spring 2026) discover:
- WOKE??
- If I were the devil
- Questions to Ask God
- The Six Elusive Virtues
- Easter versus Passover
- What is a Biblical man?
- Why do we go to Church?
- Whose Life are you Living?
- They are coming to Church!
- Socialism versus Capitalism.
- What is the Key to great Faith?
- The Blessing and Power of unity
- When the Church mirrors, the World.

www.newstartministries.ca

More Books Coming!

1. *"Prayer Pilot"* A book for people under the age of 30. How to plan your life, God's way.

2. *"Understanding Spiritual Gifts"* A book about Spiritual Gifts and provide a gift survey so you can find out what gifts God has anointed you with.

3. *"For Christian Entrepreneurs"* A book that covers what they don't teach you in secular business schools.

4. *"Understanding God's Calendar"* If we align ourselves with God's calendar, then we receive His new revelations and blessings every month!

5. *"A Study of the Six Elusive Virtues"* How much do you know about brokenness, tenderness, contriteness, meekness, humility, and gentleness?

Shopping and Seminars!

Books:
Available from Amazon, Indigo/Chapters, Barnes & Noble, or order from your favourite bookstore via Ingram Sparks.

1. *"Biblical Economics 101: Living Under God's Financial Blessing."*
2. *"Life is a Test: Hope in a Confusing World"* - Volume One
3. *"Life is a Test: Hope in a Confusing World"* - Volume Two
4. *"Life is a Test: Hope in a Confusing World"* - Volume Three
5. *"Life is a Test: Hope in a Confusing World"* - Volume Four
6. *"Life is a Test: Hope in a Confusing World"* - Volume Five (publishing date is late 2026)
7. *"Miracle Mornings: 31 Days of Declarations & Devotions"*

Posters:
Available from New Start Ministries for download.
www.newstartministries.ca

Teaching, Seminars and Consulting:

Invite Dr. Watkins to your church, conference or business event!
Pastors, would you and your church like to sponsor a seminar and have Dr. Watkins teach? Consult with you and your board? Then book a Biblical Economics 101 weekend. This seminar is perfect for those who wish to:

- Get out of unnecessary debt.
- Build kingdom wealth.
- Break free from a scarcity and poverty mentality?
- Break the mindset that to be a good Christian, you must be broke and poor.
- Destroy the lie that if we love God, we must commit to a life of poverty.
- Learn how wealth and a heart for Jesus go hand-in-hand and are not mutually exclusive.
- Understand finances through the laws of seedtime and harvest and how tithing can change your finances.

Learn about:
- False Ideas about Money
- The Purpose of Money

- Does God want you to be Blest? (yes, and out of debt too!)
- God's Economy
- A Study of Wealth and Success
- The Way to Prosperity

The schedule for a Biblical Economics 101 weekend is usually 3 hours Friday night, all day Saturday (12 hours' worth in total of teaching!) and then a message at your Sunday service if you desire. Dr. Watkins can come a few days early or stay a few days after the seminar for individual financial consulting, free of charge.

Dr. Watkins does not charge for teaching his courses, but requests two love offerings be taken for his ministry. As a church, you can charge for the seminar or host it for free.

– TESTIMONIAL –

"The conference and teaching on Biblical Principles of Economics was excellent. Everything was supported and documented with Scriptures. I always appreciate the Word of truth being opened up to us in a way like you did, in your presentation of principles for prospering. We thought your presentation was very sound and so good that we gave each of our five children a copy of the Biblical Economics 101 book for Christmas. Thank you for your research and experience."

- Alec and Ginny Wade
His Call Ministries, Midwest Regional
Apostolic Center, Sparta, MO USA

Additional Teaching Courses:
- Spiritual Gifts (including an individual survey for participants)
- Operating in the Courts of Heaven
- Healing
- Deliverance
- Spiritual Mapping and Cleansing of the Land

For a complete updated list, go to www.newstartministries.ca

Discover Inspirational Posters That Transforms Your Space - and Your Spirit.

Over the past few years, Holy Spirit stirred in my heart a vision: to create a series of powerful Christian posters that carry more than words and designs - they carry life. These twelve posters are not just artwork for your wall; they are declarations of faith, daily reminders of God's promises, and visual anchors of truth that will uplift you and everyone who walks into your home, office, classroom, or church.

We live in a world filled with noise, distraction, and discouragement. That is why it matters what you surround yourself with. The messages we see daily shape the way we think, the atmosphere we live in, and ultimately, the choices we make. These posters are designed to replace fear with faith, discouragement with hope, and confusion with clarity. Each one is a Spirit-breathed message that speaks into your heart, reminding you that God is present, faithful, and still working in your life.

Whether displayed in a living room, study, workplace, youth centre, or sanctuary, these posters bring more than decoration - they bring transformation. They are conversation starters, teaching tools, and visual reminders of eternal truth. One glance can strengthen weary faith. One Word from God can shift an atmosphere. When you fill your environment with the promises of Scripture, you are making space for God's presence to dwell.

Every poster has been prayerfully crafted with excellence, clarity, and spiritual depth. Out of the twelve available, ten are completely original works inspired by the Spirit, one was adapted (with permission) from a respected author, and one was transformed from a secular concept into a Christ-centred truth. Together, they form a collection that speaks to every aspect of life - faith, calling, finances, identity, and purpose.

Imagine the encouragement of seeing God's truth on your walls every single day. Imagine your children growing up with Scripture and Spirit-filled reminders in their rooms. Imagine your co-workers, students, or congregation walking past a poster that ignites a spark of faith in their hearts. That's the power of this collection - it doesn't just decorate a space; it changes the atmosphere and points people toward Christ.

The best part? These posters are accessible, affordable, and adaptable. Each one is available for only $9.99 as a high-quality PDF file, (B & W) ready for you to print in any size that suits your space.

www.newstartministries.ca

Frame them, laminate them, or print them on canvas - the choice is yours. You'll find them in the "Store" section of my website under "Purchase Posters and Study Guide." It's never been easier to bring beauty, Scripture, and encouragement into your environment.

Here is a closer look at each design:

1. God By Design
Created with today's youth in mind, this poster explains how and why God created you - and the divine purpose behind your existence.

2. What Is Faith?
Packed with 15 Bible references, this poster provides a clear, Scripture-based explanation of what faith truly is.

3. The Fruit of the Spirit
This design clarifies the difference between spiritual gifts and fruit, then lists every Fruit of the Spirit in a way that brings clarity and encouragement.

4. This Is Your Life
Often purchased by school counsellors and youth leaders, this poster gives young people a life-shaping perspective on what life is really about.

5. What Is Your Mission Impossible?
A companion to the *"This Is Your Life"* poster, this piece uses 12 biblical references to describe the mission each believer carries.

6. What God Says About Money
Drawn from the insights of my book, "Biblical Economics 101: Living Under God's Financial Blessing," this poster delivers God's perspective on finances and answers questions you've always had about money.

7. How To Be Rich, God's Way
A practical companion to the previous design, this poster provides a blueprint for stewarding finances God's way.

8. Jesus Was Beyond Wealth
Written by my mentor, Australian billionaire Christian businessman Dr. Peter Daniels, this design reveals the true meaning of wealth through the life of Christ.

www.newstartministries.ca

9. What Spiritual Gifts Has God Given You?
This poster lists 30 spiritual gifts, each supported by biblical references, and organizes them into the five-fold ministry framework.

10. The 10 Stages in the Life of a Christian Entrepreneur
Unlike secular teachings on entrepreneurship, this poster gives believers a Spirit-led roadmap for building a business with Kingdom purpose.

11. The Christian Life Commandments
A collection of 25 commandments from Scripture, each with its own reference, showing you how to live a successful and Christ-centred life.

12. The Blessing
Perfect for weddings, graduations, dedications, and even as a framed centerpiece in your home, this timeless design declares God's blessing over lives and families.

Each of these posters was designed with one goal in mind: to infuse your life and your environment with the Word of God. They are more than paper and ink - they are carriers of truth that will inspire, teach, and remind you daily of who God is and who you are in Him.

If you are serious about creating an atmosphere where faith flourishes and God's presence is welcomed, these posters are for you. They make excellent personal resources, unforgettable gifts, and powerful tools for ministry. Whether you are a parent, teacher, pastor, entrepreneur, or simply someone who longs to see more of God's Word shaping your life, you will find something in this collection that speaks directly to your heart.

Now is the time to invest in what truly lasts. For less than the cost of a meal, you can bring eternal words into your home, office, or church. Don't settle for empty walls when you can fill your space with truth that builds faith and transforms lives.

Visit my website today, go to the "Store," and order your posters. Print them, frame them, and let them speak life over you and those around you. Surround yourself with inspiration that doesn't fade, because one Word from God truly can change everything.

www.newstartministries.ca/shop

Notes:

www.ingramcontent.com/pod-product-compliance
Lightning Source LLC
Chambersburg PA
CBHW052146070526
44585CB00017B/2000